Making the colours sing

Making the colours sing

Michaela Youngson

British Library Cataloguing in Publication data

A catalogue record for this book is available
from the British Library

ISBN 1 85852 277 3

First published by Inspire
4 John Wesley Road
Werrington
Peterborough PE4 6ZP

Printed and bound in Great Britain by
Aldridge Print Group, Mitcham, Surrey

Dedication

To Sandy, Robert and Tamsin
for teaching me to see the beauty of the world
through my own eyes.

In Memory of

Lucy English

The glazier tries all her effects in the glass itself;
she sketches in glass.
She has all the colours burning round her,
singing to her to use them,
sounding all their chords.
'This looks better.' 'That is a pleasant harmony.'
'Ah! But this makes it sing!'

after Christopher Whall

Foreword

Worshipping God is a deep human instinct. The task of liturgy, in which we try to articulate our deepest desires, longings and questions about God, is to dare to speak about the unspeakable mystery of God.

In this collection of prayers, poems, hymns and liturgies, Michaela Youngson is attempting nothing less. She offers us words crafted by her own creative energy that describe life's ordinary experiences in the light of eternity. In a society that seems to have lost its collective Christian memory, this book is a valuable contribution to the search for legitimate language in which to communicate the love of God today. It is accessible, appropriate for private or public use, and is able, in its modern style, to re-express ancient truths and stories from Scripture.

Her theme is derived from the craft of the maker of stained glass windows, and as she uses this theme, she acknowledges the value not only of words but also of images in trying to articulate the truths we discern about God. She knows that the colours of glass can sing to us and to God not only of the ingenuity of humankind, but of the miracles and tragedies that infuse our everyday life. The collection is itself a window full of colour and light. Michaela Youngson's style is at once unapologetic and tentative as she searches for words to describe the mysteries of life and death; breast-feeding, children's conversation, the paradoxes of old age, a baby stillborn. Her primary text is her experience of life in the world and she offers us prayers and poems to frame this in our own prayers to God. It is a theological method and a liturgical approach that takes human experience seriously, in all its complexity. With Michaela, we look through our life experience in all its colour and glass-like fragility to see the God who is beyond, whose light illuminates the pictures of our lives.

We are not yet in a Church where a book of prayers and reflections written by a woman can pass without comment. Michaela's images of a God who at once comforts and challenges us as we make our way through life is not the kingly, lordly, remote figure of so much traditional Christian liturgy. Her God is one who will receive and recognize the sensual human experiences of weaning, bathing, loving. As these prayers are used publicly in churches and gatherings of different denominations, I trust that new images of God will be awakened and our understanding of life deepened.

In giving primacy to the stories and experiences of women, this book takes its place in the growing feminist canon of liturgical writing; and is an encouragement to lay and ordained men and women to expand our vocabulary and to pray with the spirit of adventure evident in these pages.

This book is a gift to all women, men and children who are searching for a way to talk to God that reflects life as it is really lived.

Canon Lucy Winkett
Precentor of St Paul's Cathedral, London

Acknowledgements

In thanking the following people, I am aware that I cannot list all those who have shaped my journey, inspired me and challenged me. However, I want to offer particular thanks to the people of the Burnley and the Accrington and Haslingden Methodist Circuits – for much love and for teaching me a great deal;

Beryl and David Cowling, Jenni and Bernard Whittle, and Kath and Dave Eardly for help and hospitality on our family tour of Scottish glass;

Alison Tomlin, Chris Cheeseman, Jonathan Kerry, Andrew Horsfall and Neil Stubbens – for wise words always offered at just the right time;

Lucy Winkett, Cathy Bird and Lorraine Brown – for friendship without limits and for asking hard questions;

Stephanie English – for what only a twin sister can give;

Rachel Newton, Dudley Coates and Joy Mead – for getting me writing again; and Natalie Watson at Inspire for encouragement and confidence.

Contents

Introduction

Creation

'The dullest bits of glass are the easiest to cut.'
I remember telling this to a church member as I attempted to demonstrate the art of stained glass construction at a church Christmas Fair. A flawless, regular, machine-rolled piece of glass will, with the correct cutting pressure, break along the score pretty much every time. A piece of glass with texture, bubbles, bands of colour, can confound even the most experienced artist by breaking in an unexpected way. Despite the risk, I would choose to create an image with the more 'interesting' glass every time.

A window made up of regular shapes and predictable colours can be executed perfectly and may be a great addition to an architectural design. Personally, I find more beauty in windows made up of awkward, uneven, irregular shapes – the sort of shapes needed to represent people, stories and landscapes. The best windows create a sense of other, of transcendence; pointing to something beyond ourselves and often involving risk, heartache and a sense of journeying.

This bringing together of flawed and unique elements to create something much greater than the sum of its parts has echoes in all art forms – it is also a reflection of human community. Our human community would be greatly impoverished if we were all flawless, identical and predictable. Our Creator did not desire a 'Stepford Wives' community of programmed beings living tidy and safe lives. We are offered an existence in which all the pieces do not fit easily together and each piece is unique and has its own idiosyncratic beauty. This is what makes human life a risky, challenging and profoundly beautiful work of art.

Salvation

'Are you saved?'
I'd just moved into my first manse as a Methodist minister and a woman from the village arrived at the door to ask me about the state of my soul. Personally I was more interested in finding which box the kettle had been inadvertently packed into. No matter how often I tell myself that the phrase 'are you saved?' is one branch of Christianity's shorthand for the complex and profound story of my own and humanity's relationship with God, I still find it irritating!

My answer to what lies behind that coded question would involve a book in itself. However, a few elements of the answer provide some pointers to how *Making the colours sing* came to be written.

I was 'saved' in a very practical way by attendance at my local Methodist church. It was a place where I was accepted for who I was. My youth leaders and friends there became a second family and provided a safe space for me to challenge racism and sexism and the politics which I could not challenge at home, school or, later, at work. I was offered opportunities to travel nationally and internationally, meeting people who broadened my perspective and helped me encounter God in ways that made sense of some of my experiences. At this time I wrote – poems, prose, stories – anything that expressed who I was, my questions about the world, faith and injustice. Writing helped me cope with all the ups and downs of growing and changing, as well as coming to terms with being sexually assaulted.

I stopped writing in these ways when I trained to be a minister. Apart from the time commitment to required reading and essay writing, preaching and more essays, I felt that I had to focus on 'grown up' writing. After five years in ministry I prepared to go on retreat. Part of the preparation was to write a paper about my ministry. Time after time I found myself using poetry to reflect. Tears flowed more than once as I felt a part of myself returning to life. The writing that had been a very private and, for some eight years, restricted expression of who I am, began to exist in a more public way.

I was approached to write some book reviews, local radio 'thoughts for the day', and some Bible studies and liturgies for various publications. At the same time my interest in modern stained glass grew and my own simple attempts at making windows gave me a great deal of satisfaction. Friends began to encourage me to send a proposal to a publisher and *Making the colours sing* is the outcome of taking that risk.

Inspiration

'Yes, but does it make the colours sing?'
Christopher Wahl was the acknowledged expert in the design and construction of stained glass windows at the beginning of the twentieth century. When told of a particularly good window by an apprentice Wahl's reaction was to ask, 'Yes, but does it make the colours sing?'

If you look at a stained glass window from outside it will appear dull. You may appreciate the artistry and the skill of construction but you will not see its full created potential. Only when light passes through the glass and makes the 'colours sing' does the full glory of this created work sing out. The light transforms the glass it passes through and is itself transformed by the glass, arriving within the building changed as it transforms the space into which it flows.

This transformation of an object to its full potential which, in turn, transforms the space around it, speaks profoundly of the activity of the divine Spirit in our lives.

We are each made unique, beautiful and with astonishing potential. Most of us exist, most of the time, like a window waiting for the light to break through. It is in moments of 'inspiration' when we are most in tune with the divine life force – God's Spirit – that our true potential shines out. Not only are we transformed but also we transform the people and the world around us.

These moments, events or life stages of 'inspiration' are those times when we are fully alive and catch a sense of the true created potential within us. It may be that we are not aware of living in this state of spiritual wholeness and yet others see the Creator's glory reflected in us.

What causes the 'colours to sing' in our lives? It may be the combination of a particular landscape with good food and excellent wine! It may be a piece of music, a painting, a poem or the laughter of a child. Perhaps it is one of those moments when we feel most alive because of love or being part of awe-inspiring worship; or sharing in passionate, sensitive sex. Often it is the coming together of the damaged, irregular, flawed and beautiful members of the human family into communities of shared concern, celebration and challenge.

These experiences allow a glimpse of the divine to break through the dullness with which we so often feel comfortable. Our attentiveness to the divine life in others and ourselves will help us to embrace the risky living that brings us closer to our Creator and allows God to make our colours sing.

Michaela Youngson
February 2005

Beginnings

Once upon a time ...
No, before time itself.
Okay ... Once, before time began ...
No, not once, but always, in each moment.

Once, and always and in each moment
    a story began and ended
    and yet had no beginning and no end.
The Storyteller laughed
    and in that laughter the story was born.
The heroine in the story was the Storyteller.
The story could not be told without the heroine,
    it meant nothing without her.
The laughter of the Storyteller brought life and light
    and swept up all in its chorus of joy.
Before it all darkness vanished
    and despair was denounced.
Hope, joy and love held sway
    and all laughed happily ever after.

Beginnings

In the Christian calendar stories of birth and new beginnings are caught up with Christmas and the promise of the Messiah. We are reminded that God became a human being and entered history in a particular place and time.

The introduction to John's Gospel goes far beyond beginning the story of God's saving love with the physical birth of Jesus. John locates 'The Word' with God at the beginning of all things. The very existence of all creation relies on the presence of 'the Word' with God. It is the relationship of love that is God's own existence which provides the spark that brings about creation. All things come into being because, and only because, of the creative power of love. This love has no beginning and no end; it brings hope that chases away despair.

People see birthdays and anniversaries as significant; years go by and bring change, experience and wisdom. God's nature is eternal but we need to measure our lives. Each of us has a story to tell and a journey to travel. The items in Chapter 1 are about beginnings – creation, pregnancy and birth, Advent, Christmas and the New Year.

In Genesis 1
   Work was begun
      God made the stars and the moon and the sun.
         No 'time and motion' inspectors around
            Time and motion had only just been invented.

         In Genesis 1
            Labour was born
               God gave creation shape and form.
                  With no line manager around
                     God 'self-appraised' and saw that it was good.

            In Genesis 1
               Elements were divided
                  God demarcated water and land.
                     With no arbitration services around
                        God negotiated the boundaries of wet and dry.

All in a day's work

         In Genesis 1
         Eco-systems came into being
         God made the earth the cradle of life.
         With systems analysts not yet analysing
         God drew no distinctions but thrilled in life run amuck.

         In Genesis 1
         Teamwork was conceived
         God needed help.
         With human resources not being ready
         God created a workforce and gave them a job description.

         In Genesis 1
         The working week was invented
         God understood the value of production.
         With no contracts necessary
         God gave the command to 'go forth and multiply'.

      In Genesis 2
         Maximum working hours were initiated
         God took a day off.
         With no guilt at missed deadlines
         God blessed, hallowed and rested from all the work of creation.

Loved into life

A movement, a flutter
a sound in utter
silence.

From nothing
from no thing
life.

Take absence
void of sense
and touch.

Make love.
Create space.
Take risk.

Into the empty silence
bring singing, dancing,
longing, birthing,
dying, weeping.

From your deep well of creative laughter,
bring life,
flowing, pouring, gushing,
springing, refreshing.

Birth-giver,
ancient dancer,
move with the rhythm
of all you have made.

Story-weaver,
tell us again
how it is very good
and how you love us into life.

A pregnant pause

Creator God,
from time before time
until time beyond time,
your whole being has been pregnant with possibilities.
You bring solar systems into existence
    and pour your life-giving Spirit into the fabric of creation.

For a while, I have a taste,
    a sense, an inkling of your true nature
    as I create space in my own body for life to grow.

Do you feel this incredible excitement,
    this high anxiety, this wonder and fear
    as you contemplate the myriad lives
    you have shaped and created?

Do you know the nausea,
    the sleepless nights, the worry and care
    that I experience in anticipation of this child's birth?

Do you know the love, fiercely strong,
    awesome in breadth
    and sweet beyond words
        that is growing deep within
        as I wait to hold this baby of mine?

Pour out your love,
    your protection,
    your Spirit,
    that this pregnancy will go well.
Hold in your care all who bear life
    and all who share with them in the wonder of creation.
                        Amen.

Blessing

Bless pregnant women everywhere
    those who are joyful and those who know great fear and pain.

Bless husbands, lovers and partners
    those who share in creating new life.

Bless midwives, doctors and helpers
    those who care for mother and child.

Bless mothers, sisters, aunties and friends
    those who tell stories of birthing and courage and love.

Bless those who cannot conceive and those who choose not to;
    grant them comfort and strength.

Bless those whose babies and children are unable to live;
    grant healing and hope.

Bless communities and nations with the vision and courage
    to value children and to work for their well-being.
                           Amen.

Advent intercessions

Week 1

Leader: Let us pray to the God of Sarah and Abraham, of Ruth, David, and all our mothers and fathers in faith.

To those who face an uncertain future, refugees, asylum seekers, prisoners of conscience;
All: God of promise, send your peace.

Leader: To those who long for children
and for children who long for parents;
All: God of promise, send your peace.

Leader: To those who take the risk of following your call;
All: God of promise, send your peace.

Leader: To those who struggle in their relationships;
All: God of promise, send your peace.

Leader: To those who have waited long years
to see the fruit of their labours for you;
All: God of promise, send your peace.

Leader: We thank you for those ordinary, flawed human beings
who have set before us an example of faith and obedience.
As you accept our prayers for others;
All: help us to respond to your call. Amen

Week 2

Leader: Let us pray to God for those who wait in darkness.

To those who long for the dawn's light,
whose nights are full of fear and unrest;

All: **Gracious God, send your light to a dark world.**

Leader: To those who long for an end to pain,
waiting for healing or death's quiet release;

All: **Gracious God, send your light to a dark world.**

Leader: To those who worship money, possessions and status,
with little understanding of how dark their lives have become;

All: **Gracious God, send your light to a dark world.**

Leader: To those who endure poverty's endless night
and watch helpless as their children suffer;

All: **Gracious God, send your light to a dark world.**

Leader: To those whose lives are full of grief,
who carry the wounds of great loss;

All: **Gracious God, send your light to a dark world.**

Leader: To those who have no hope and cannot see any way ahead;

All: **Gracious God, send your light to a dark world.**

Leader: The God who hears our prayers sends a messenger saying,
'Those who walk in darkness have seen a great light.'

All: **Thanks be to God. Amen.**

Week 3

Leader: Let us pray to the God of Elizabeth, Zechariah
          and John the Baptist.

          To those who have lost hope of new life,
          whose faith has become no more than habit-bound religion;
All: **God of truth, send your message of hope.**

Leader: To those who have no faith
          and are troubled by an emptiness of spirit;
All: **God of truth, send your message of hope.**

Leader: To those who exist at the margins of life,
          in the wilderness of poverty and powerlessness;
All: **God of truth, send your message of hope.**

Leader: To those who seek a new beginning,
          who long for forgiveness and the chance to start again;
All: **God of truth, send your message of hope.**

Leader: To those who answer the calling to be prophets
          in a world deaf to justice and peace;
All: **God of truth, send your message of hope.**

Leader: John the Baptizer proclaimed the presence of God's son,
          and called to repentance those who held power in the land;
All: **God of truth, encourage our witness and accept our prayers.
          Amen.**

Week 4

Leader: Let us pray to the God of Mary, the Mother of Jesus.
To those who, though afraid, respond to your call with joy;

All: Life-giving God, send your gentle Spirit.

Leader: To those who wait for life to begin,
who look for the next big chance
and miss the potential in each moment;

All: Life-giving God, send your gentle Spirit.

Leader: To those who bear their children in poverty,
and fear for their lives;

All: Life-giving God, send your gentle Spirit.

Leader: To those who are forced to travel, to flee or to hide;

All: Life-giving God, send your gentle Spirit.

Leader: To those who cannot understand or accept the lifestyles
and choices of their children;

All: Life-giving God, send your gentle Spirit.

Leader: God, our life-giver, merciful and gentle,
you chose a brave young woman
to bring your light into this world.

**All: Help us to say 'Yes' when you call us into your service
and accept our prayers in the name of Jesus. Amen.**

Christmas

Opening responses

Leader: Gather round, come closer, there is no reason to fear the dark.
All: **The light of the world shines in our hearts.**

Leader: Come and worship, the waiting is over, the gift of love is given.
All: **The light of the world shines in our hearts.**

Leader: Look! Look and see all our hope, become real in a tiny child.
All: **The light of the world shines in our hearts.**

Leader: Let us worship God with wonder, awe and joy!
All: **The light of the world shines in our hearts.**

Confession

Leader: We have longed for the dawn
but never believed it would come:
All: **Loving God, forgive us.**

Leader: We have seen signs of your arrival
but failed to understand them:
All: **Loving God, forgive us.**

Leader: We expected the Messiah
but thought he would arrive in power and might:
All: **Loving God, forgive us.**

Leader: We looked for you
but we looked in the palaces of the wealthy:
All: **Loving God, forgive us.**

Leader: God of new birth and new beginnings,
we thank you that you forgive all our sins.
Help us to look for you in all places and all people.
All: **In the name of Jesus, Amen.**

Welcome
Jesus Christ

We've decked our halls with boughs of holly,
    and tinsel, streamers, cards, pictures of Santa ...
We've marked the season to be jolly,
    with booze and food and promises to keep in touch.
We've sung the carols and watched the plays,
    nativities and pantomimes – Oh yes we have!
We've queued in supermarket lines,
    and realized that we've forgotten the sprouts.

We are ready, we are really ready.
Well, come on then, Christmas, do your stuff,
    make us happy, merry, jolly!

Well, come on Christmas.
Welcome Christmas
Welcome Christ.

Welcome Christ, welcome baby Jesus,
    join in the party, the celebration.
We are ready for you now.

Here is warm and prickly straw.
Here are soft swaddling bands.
Here is a world which needs you, little baby.
Here are our hearts – make us your manger.
Here are our lives – make us your Bethlehem.
Here is your Church – make us your Body.

Welcome Jesus Christ.

New Year prayer of praise

Creator God, we praise you
> for this New Year,
> for this time of worship,
> for this moment in our lives.

Creator God, we praise you
> for all that you have made,
> for all that you have given,
> for all that you have promised.

Redeemer God, we praise you
> for the new life found in Christ,
> for the chance to begin again,
> for the story of salvation.

Redeemer God, we praise you
> for your grace that is without limit,
> for your love which knows no end,
> for your living among us.

Sustainer God, we praise you
> for the gift of your Spirit,
> for the outpouring of your love,
> for the fruits of our relationship with you.

Sustainer God, we praise you
> for your open embrace of all,
> for your infectious joy,
> for your presence in our lives.

Amen.

Dedicated to the 'New Year fearers'

When Auld acquaintance has 'bin' forgot
and the debris of another midnight madness
cleared away,
out will come the New Year fearers
the January first pain bearers
the hogmanay haters
and tremendous fun traitors
who do not see why
they should even try
to get plastered
or blasted
for the sake
of one more day on the calendar
and one more year gone by.

On will be put the brave faces
that remember the places
of memory and grief
no nostalgia will bring relief
from the constant reminders
of long-gone lovers
lost opportunities
and broken communities.

'Happy New Year!'
Shed another tear
move on through the winter
that freezes hope's last splinter
of consolation.
Each sharp inhalation
of breath is a cold effort
of courage in the face
of despair.
One more cheerful mask
is added to the growing collection
as the lonely New Year fearer
looks for a different benediction.

Letting go

A reflection on weaning

It has been such a privilege, being able to give you all that you have needed for life. For nine months you formed and grew, you moved and lived and our bodies were as one. Then birth, hard work and painful for me – traumatic and frightening for you. The letting go began.

I had to learn to share you, to make space for others to love you and hold you. I delighted in their love of you, but I was always glad when they handed you back.

Breast-feeding was amazing. There were those first nervous days when we got to know what worked best for us. Finding the right positions, how to be modest without compromising my declared position: 'If anyone has a problem with this, it's their problem!' Again, I could give you all you needed and the joy of you feeding and looking into my eyes defies description. Then you began to look around you and your world grew bigger and more diverse each day.
The letting go continued.

You started to want more than I could give. This is a good thing, I know. In my mind I know that loving you is about creating space for you to grow. My heart, however, is less rational and longs to hold on to those early moments of completeness. But if my selfish heart were to have its way how could your dad know the joy of feeding you, the joy of knowing what it is to give you life?
The letting go continued.

My heart was moved to recognize the sense of weaning about the same time as you grew your first teeth! You are being equipped with the tools and skills that will allow you to get on in the world without your dad and me. Growing up is about so much more than acquiring independence. It is about adventure and experiment, about mistakes and being forgiven, accepted and loved. I know that loving you will be about letting you go. My hope is that you will want to share your life's adventure with me and that letting go will free us both to be happy and whole.

Growing up

Bright colours
formed in simple shapes
framing life's joyful picture.
Sticky fingers,
itching to touch
to reach new things.
Fishing for the treasure of living
with the exuberance
of childhood's freedom.
Instinctively knowing God,
in creation and in people.
Giggling with generous laughter
and buoyant with the knowledge of God's blessing.

Growing up

'I wish I was a child again but with all the knowledge I have now!' The flaw with such thinking is that it is those things we have acquired as we grow up that stop us being like the little ones that Jesus welcomed. Children have an instinctive knowledge of God and a natural relationship with God. All too often we 'unlearn' what we know of God as we are taught the values and prejudices of our adult life.

Jesus did not invite the little ones to prove a point to the disciples or the crowd. Jesus listened to the children and blessed them because he loved them and wanted them to know that they were valued and precious to God.

Growing up is an adventure; it is an exciting and risky business. We can be tempted to rush the process, encouraging children to see the world through adult eyes before they are ready. Childhood should be a safe time and space in which to have fun, to learn, to experiment and push at boundaries.

The poems, reflections and prayers in this chapter attempt to celebrate childhood. Most are inspired by Robert and Tamsin, my wise, adventurous, funny and loving children. We do not all live with children in our lives, some wish they could, others choose not to – but we have all been children and we are all God's children.

'Let the little ones come to me, for God's garden belongs to such as these. They understand the invitation and the gift. It is true that you cannot enter the garden unless you too understand the gift as these children do.'

(Luke 18.16-17, paraphrase)

How did God make toilets?

A dialogue between Tamsin, aged four, and Mummy

Tamsin: Mummy, how did God make toilets?

Mummy: Well, God didn't actually make toilets.

Tamsin: But you said that God made everything!

Mummy: Ye...s, God made all the things that we use to make other things with.

Tamsin: Pardon?

Mummy: Well, God made the minerals that people have learned to use to turn into toilets.

Tamsin: What are minerwals?

Mummy: Minerals are found in rocks and can be used for all sorts of things.

Tamsin: So how did God make minerals?

Mummy: We...ll, when God breathed the universe into being – no scratch that. Erm, God is able to do anything because God is pure love and very mysterious.

Tamsin: Oh, so how did God make curtains?

Mummy: Ooh look, here comes Daddy!

It's not fair!

A dialogue between Robert, aged nine, and Mum (ageing rapidly)

Robert: Mum, you know you told Tamsin that God could do anything?

Mum: Yes.

Robert: Well, why do children die because there's not enough food?

Mum: There is enough food but God has given people freedom to make choices and because some people are selfish and greedy or don't care, others go hungry.

Robert: But that's not fair! The hungry people don't have the choice. If God can do anything, why do some people die of diseases that we can cure?

Mum: Again, there are some people and companies that want to make lots of profit and poor countries can't afford the drugs they need.

Robert: But that's not fair! Why doesn't God make all the greedy people kind?

Mum: Then we would be like puppets or robots and God wants us to grow and learn by experience – not by being programmed like a computer.

Robert: Sounds to me like God's not much use and we are going to have to sort this mess out ourselves.

Mum: It's when we ask questions like these and realize it's up to us that God is working in the world through us.

Robert: Yeah, yeah. I still don't understand why God doesn't sort things out quickly and stop wars and famine and all that.

Mum: I have to admit that I don't know all the answers.

Robert: Okay, can I ask you another question?

Mum: (Gulps) Yes, of course.

Robert: Can I go and play on my Game Boy?

Mum: What a good idea!

At a safe distance

You run ahead
in the park
with all the careless
freedom of being five.

You run ahead until,
stop!
You see the squirrel
in its search for summer's store.
You move slowly,
carefully,
instinctively
knowing
how close you can get
before the nut-gatherer
will run,
bounding to a safe distance.

Nothing else exists.
In such moments
the whole universe
consists
of you
and that squirrel;
you and that game
of stalking and
trusting and
giggling.
I stand outside
your universe
at a safe distance.

Today
we took
the top path

In our park there is a green gradient
of well-trimmed grass.
At its boundary trees offer shade
on lazy walks home from school.

Today we took the top path
looking down over the green lawn
and beyond to the red and grey town
shimmering below.
Side by side, Robert and I;
my ears rang with the non-stop
details of the last few hours.

You had gone ahead, Tamsin,
running, giggling
and turning handstands into tipple-tails.
Zigzagging in between the trees;
playing the now predictable
'where am I' game of hide-and-seek.

As you jumped
from behind each tree in turn,
I gasped.
For each footstep,
each noisy, clattering
chattering explosion of life,
was heralded by nature's dancers.
A cloud of butterflies
fluttered up,
flew a few feet ahead,
and landed again
to soak up the afternoon sun.
My whirlwind daughter
squealing and spinning
danced with delight.
Abandoning her wistful game
she joined the butterflies
in their dance.
All else became other,
existed beyond the boundaries
and steps of
the Painted Lady Polka.

Children's prayers

Praise

You are so amazing, God.
You made our world and the moon, the sun,
    the stars and the planets.
You are so amazing, God.
You made rivers and plants, animals and insects.
You are so amazing, God.
You made every person different and special.
You are so amazing, God.
You sent Jesus to help us to know how to live.
You are so amazing, God.
You're really cool!

                              Amen.

Thanksgiving

We thank God for mornings when we walk to school
    through rustling crunchy leaves.
We thank God for squirrels and birds in the park.
We thank God for rainbows and all the colours in the world.
We thank God for friends to play with and families who love us.

                              Amen.

Thank you, God, for today

Thank you for all the things I'll do, the people I will meet.
Thank you for the things I will learn, the games I'll play.
Thank you for food I will eat.
Thank you for loving me.

                                        Amen.

Confession

I had to say 'sorry' a lot today.
Sorry to Dad for leaving my shoes where he could trip over them.
Sorry to my sister for ignoring her.
Sorry to my friend for shouting at him.
Sorry to Mum for not setting the table.

So you see, God, I've said 'sorry' a lot today.
Everyone forgave me and that made me feel better
      and made me want to try harder.
So I'm saying 'sorry' to you as well
      because Jesus said you would forgive me.
Thank you for forgiving me and could you help me
      'get out of bed on the right side' tomorrow?
                                        Amen.

Prayers for others

Dear God,
I watched the news today,
there was a huge earthquake in a country called ....
Lots of people died and were hurt and haven't anywhere to live.
Please help those people.

Amen.

Dear God,
Can you help?
My gran's not well and people keep talking in whispers.
I don't really understand what's going on.
Please help her to get better.

Amen.

Dear God,
My mum says we can't have sweets made by a big company.
She says they don't pay their workers properly.
Please will you help people who are poor.
Help big companies to do the right thing.
And please help me not mind having other sweets instead.

Amen.

the hight o' what's wyss
is the dred o' the Lord

Growing

awareness

I begin to leave childish ways.
The comfortable laughter
of early days fades, replaced by knowledge
of a world larger than before.
Unfairness, bigotry,
a complex system of economy
where my actions impact on other lives.
I have choices to make,
ethical, social, radical, liberal.
How do others see me?
How do I see myself?
Where is God in the complex,
messy, unfair world?

Growing awareness

Adolescence and early adult life is a time when the certainties of childhood are replaced by questions about our identity, the world we live in and, for people of faith, what it means to live as God's children.

It is now that we are most sharply aware of prejudice and injustice. It is an age when we believe that hypocrisy is the worst of all crimes and the Jesus we relate to tells off the hypocrites, turns the tables in the Temple and offers a place in God's home for women, for sinners and for the poor. The paraphrase of Matthew 23.13-36 expresses something of the adolescent's simple fury against phoney religion.

The items in this chapter reflect my own journey into awareness. As a twin I have always had a powerful aversion to injustice, particularly mistaken identity films! But in my early working life and as I looked at the Church and the world, my understanding of the exclusion of women deepened. This is reflected in the items focusing on the way the stories of Old Testament women do not offer a full picture of their lives.

'On Eagle's Wings' is a hymn based on Isaiah 40.21-31 and is a reminder that there is hope in God who created all life. It points out that those who rule the earth hold power for a very short time and was written as powerful nations planned war without the authority of the world community. In the face of the horrors of war we can feel very small and inadequate to the task of bringing good news to those who need it. It is good to be reminded that 'God's love makes us fly like eagles, renews our strength and will not let us fall; so we shall run, no cause will make us feeble. The faithful of all ages, caught up in God's call.'

Who's telling the story?

As the waters flowed from Eden,
forming four great rivers,
so flow the tears of generations of women.

The River Pishon meandered through the land of Havilah,
a land of gold, sweet-scented resin and onyx.
The River Gihon sparkled across the entire land of Cush.

The great Tigris ran along the east of Asshur and the mighty Euphrates brought life and refreshment to those who dwelt on its banks.

At the source of these rivers, so the ancient story goes, a man had too much work to do, tending God's garden and naming all living creatures. God understood the need to live in relationship, having enjoyed living in community since before time began. It was no great deed for the creator of all to alter her plans and make for the man a partner, a companion, a lover and friend.

In the woman creation was complete, finished, perfect. She was the icing on the divine cake. The man knew that she was part of him and he part of her; there was to be no separation.

However, this did not suit the storyteller. Such harmony did not explain the imperfections in the world in which he lived. Life was not a garden where noisy, careless, joyful children danced and sang. Reality was hard and full of conflict. The storyteller had to use harsh words such as sin and evil to sum up the world as he saw it.

This was not good news; the story seemed to begin well – perfection, harmony (he had forgotten that the true beginning lay in chaos). How did things get in such a mess? There was only one thing to do – find someone to blame, write in a scapegoat! But who would it be?

The woman, of course – after all, she arrived later than the man and the storyteller was male, so it stands to reason that she should be blamed for the whole hideous mess. The storyteller understood temptation and wrote it in graphic detail into the story; he knew women, how easily they wrapped men around their little fingers, how they wanted power and to know everything. It didn't take a lot of imagination for that storyteller.

And so it began.

First blame, then brutality, then banishment. The storyteller felt a bit uncomfortable about the way the woman was portrayed, so he kept her story small, hidden under the great and mighty doings of men. Other storytellers took over, men telling their tales round the campfires, as the women busied themselves with chores.

The women would tell their own stories, with great gusts of laughter and much gesticulation. Sometimes they would talk quietly, sharing secrets and whispering the mysteries of womankind to their daughters.

Later the male storytellers became learned, they could write their stories on papyrus, parchment and paper. The stories gained a new status; deviation from the approved text became a crime. The women's voices were not heard by the scribes given authority over the words of law, prophecy and revelation.

And so it continued.
As the waters flowed from Eden,
forming four great rivers,
so flow the tears of generations of women.

We who have received the stories need to honour the silenced women of his-story. The art of reading between the lines, filling in the gaps, is not easy – we will be condemned even for trying. But it will be worth the effort, recapturing the dreams and life-stories of our foremothers will enlighten us about ourselves and will ensure that our daughters' voices are heard in the stories of the future.

What is your story?

What is your story, Sarai?
A beautiful woman, traded to Pharaoh by your husband's fear.
Bitter barrenness confounded as Yahweh prompted laughter
and promised a nation from your womb.
A jealous mother, sending your husband's son into a barren wilderness
that still divides his children today.

What is your story, Hagar?
Egyptian maidservant, Abram's second wife,
suffering ill-treatment at Sarah's hands.
You received messages from angels, Yahweh's promise of a great nation.
Exiled and abandoned by those you served,
yet protected and loved by God.

What is your story, Dinah?
Daughter of Leah and Israel.
Raped and bartered for by a prince.
A possession to be used in trickery, torture, pillage and plunder.

What is your story, Tamar?
Widowed wife of Judah's two unrighteous sons.
Intelligent woman who tricked Judah and gave birth to twins.

What is your story, Deborah?
A wise women, a prophetess and judge in Israel.
You led your nation and held court in Ephraim.
You commanded an army and spoke God's words.

What is your story, Jael?
Nomad, friend of kings and judges.
You lured Sisera, tricked him and killed him.
Your name lives on in Deborah's Song.

What is your story, unnamed women of Judges 19?
Concubine to a Levite, welcomed by a stranger.
Sent out by your husband to be raped in his stead.
Dissected by your husband and sent to the 12 tribes as a call to war.

What is your story, Rahab?
Did you sell out your people as you sold your body?
What happened after Jericho fell
and you and your loved ones were spared?

What is your story, Miriam?
Offering childcare to save your brother.
Dancing with joy at your people's victory
and punished for wanting the same access to Yahweh
that Moses enjoyed.

What are your stories, Merab and Michal?
Daughters of Saul.
We know so much about Jonathan your brother.
Michal you married and loved David and saved his life.

What is your story, Abigail?
An intelligent and beautiful woman,
you outsmarted your surly, mean husband and,
once widowed, became David's wife.

What are your stories, Medium of Endor, Wise Women of Tekoa and Abel?
What are your stories, concubines of David's palace, used by Absalom?
What are your stories, Rizpah, Abishag, Vashti and Gomer?
What are your stories ...
What are your stories?

Banquet diplomacy

It was a good living but hard work being a cook in King Xerxes' court. We got some really interesting ingredients to work with because His Majesty had 127 provinces sending tribute. From India to Persia, Media to Cush, and some other more unpronounceable places – all sending dignitaries to our palace here in Susa.

Xerxes really knew how to throw a bash! After three years on the throne he thought it was time to show off a bit, and, my word, could he strut his stuff? For 180 days the wealth of his kingdom was on display, including his concubines and Her Majesty, Queen Vashti. She was getting mighty sick of it all after the first six months. It must be hard work keeping up appearances for all that time!

Well, after the 180 days were over the King threw a banquet. Not your standard royal supper of 20 odd courses, oh no! This banquet lasted for seven days and it was huge. Everyone was there in the garden of the palace. When I say 'everyone' I don't mean the women – the only women there were servants like me. Oh, the splendour defies description. The gardens were draped with white and blue linen tied to marble pillars with purple and white linen cords, fixed to silver rings. There were couches of gold and silver on pavements made of delicate mosaics. Wine was served from goblets of gold, each one unique. The King's hospitality was already legendary but no one had ever seen so much food or witnessed so much wine flowing.

Her Majesty also gave a banquet for the women in her own quarters in the palace. This was a little more civilized – I think she was worn out after months of parading her splendour in front of visitors from here, there and everywhere. Anyway, after a week of hard partying, the King was somewhat giddy with wine and a bit bored. He ordered the seven eunuchs who served him to bring Queen Vashti before him wearing her royal crown, so he could display her incredible beauty to the nobles.

So, off went the seven servants, only to be refused! Vashti was not willing to be paraded before a load of drunken dignitaries. I'm not sure why, but the gossip around the palace was that she had gone to bed with a headache and looked far from her usual gorgeous self.

The King was beside himself with anger. He spat out orders, demanding all his counsellors and legal experts advise him what must be done. It didn't take long for the seven law-makers of the Medes and Persians to reach a decision. They were rattled because they thought if Vashti got away with this then women throughout the kingdom would hear of it and refuse to obey their husbands.

Some of the married women who work in the kitchens chuckled for ages when they heard this – it would seem that most of them worked out ways of ignoring their husbands without them realizing it years ago!

Vashti wasn't laughing, though. She was banished from the King's sight for life and was no longer Queen – they decided to find someone who would do the job better.

The King and his nobles seemed quite cheerful after making this decision but thought they had better make sure that the women of the land knew their place. The King sent heralds to all parts of the kingdom, to tell each people in their own language that every man should be ruler in his own household. This being the law of the Medes and Persians it cannot be repealed – for all time. Personally, I'm not convinced that it's up to the King how people get on in their homes. I think I'll stay single and carry on working at the palace – I reckon it's a lot less work than getting married!

Women put in their place

Esther 1

Seven days for Susa's people;
seven days for great and small;
seven days of pomp and splendour,
    of gold and marble, mother of pearl.

Seven days of banquet's bounty;
seven days of full flagon's fine;
seven days of pavements of porphyry,
    of silver, mosaic and royal wine.

Seven eunuchs to bring Vashti;
seven eunuchs convey command;
seven eunuchs to show Queen's beauty,
    yet return with empty hand.

Seven sages, Medes and Persians;
seven sages, counsels sought;
seven sages give their version
    of the law that rules in court.

Seven sages before the King;
seven sages please Susa's men;
seven sages wisdom bring
    put women in their place again.

Esther's song

Mordecai, my Father, my cousin,
my heart is full of love for you.
I praise God for the wisdom granted
    to you,
I praise God for the mercy granted to me.

Mordecai, you led me from our home,
You placed me in the courts of a
    mighty ruler.
I praise God for the beauty of my eyes,
I praise God for the grace of my body.

I entered the pampering house of
    royal vanity,
massaged with myrrh and olive oil,
prepared with perfumes and taught to
    wear my beauty well,
I was ready to win favour with the King.

My King crowned me with a
    golden crown,
an awesome weight of responsibility
rested upon my head,
and I carried my people in my heart.

Cousin, you saved my husband
from the conspirators' knives,
little knowing that this would bring life
to Yahweh's children.

I despise the plotter, Haman.
He would have you and our people
bow before him, idolatrous fool.
He knows not our devotion to God.

He was a danger, a threat to all
Israel's children in these lands.
We could not allow his cruel treachery,
our only hope was a King's mercy.

Trembling inside, I approached
    my husband,
my life forfeit if he did not welcome me.
He offered his gold sceptre of grace
and my plan for salvation took form.

Vashti refused to join the King's
    banquet.
Now my people's lives depended on
    the King
and Haman banqueting within
    my quarters.
Still they did not know my story.

One banquet more would settle
    the score,
declaring the traitor's infamy.
I praise God for the plan
that saved my people and ended
    this harm.

Praise God for the lots cast in memory.
Praise God for the courage given to
    this girl Queen.
Praise God for the greatness of a
    faithful man.
Praise God for the union of Xerxes and
    Esther.

Proverbs 8.1-10 revisited

Does not woman call out?
Does not the sister raise her voice?
In the hills on her journey, where paths meet,
    she takes her stand;
Beside the gates of the city, the city that is man's domain,
    she takes her stand.
At the entrances (beyond which she finds no admittance)
    she cries aloud:
'To you, oh men, I call out; I raise my voice to you all.
    You, who are selfish, gain love.
    You, who are rapists, learn trust.
    You, who are patronisingly pious, learn truth.
    You, who have robbed me of my self-respect,
        gain your own dignity.
    You, who have chained me to fields, sinks, mundane chores
      and cheated me of my birthright,
        gain your own fullness of life.
    You, who have used language to reinforce domination over me,
      gain new words.
    You, who are blind to my needs, gain sight.
Listen, for I have worthy things to say:
I open my lips to speak what is right.
My mouth speaks what is true.
Choose my release, my fulfilment above silver,
    justice above pure gold.
For woman is more precious than rubies,
    and nothing you desire,
      nothing that you seek, in your limited vision,
        can compare with her.'

Turning the tables

Confession

Reader: 'My house shall be a house of prayer;
but you have made it a den of robbers.'

Leader: Gracious God, when we use religion for our own profit:

All: Forgive us and renew your Spirit within us.

Reader: 'My house shall be a safe place;
but you have made it a place of prejudice.'

Leader: Gracious God, when we use Scripture to support division:

All: Forgive us and renew your Spirit within us.

Reader: 'My house shall be an open space;
but you have made it a place of rigid rules.'

Leader: Gracious God, when we use dogma
to prevent others growing in their faith:

All: Forgive us and renew your Spirit within us.

Reader: 'My house shall be a healing place;
but you have made it a place of pain.'

Leader: Gracious God, when we cause hurt
and injury to ourselves and others:

All: Forgive us and renew your Spirit within us.

Reader: 'My house shall be a holy space;
but you have made it place of death and decay.'

Leader: Gracious God, when we fail to value our faith properly:

All: Forgive us and renew your Spirit within us.

Silence

Leader: Jesus burned with the desire
that all might worship in Spirit and truth;
and through him we are offered new life.
Know in your hearts that you are forgiven.

All: Thanks be to God. Amen.

Loving God and our neighbour

Confession

Holy God, your Son showed us by his life and through his teaching,
what it means to love you with our whole being
and to love our neighbours as ourselves.

We have become selfish with the gifts you have granted;
remind us of the generosity that you require of us.

We have feasted well at the expense of the poor;
remind us of the justice that you require of us.

We have closed our doors to those who seem different;
remind us of the hospitality that you require of us.

We have used words to justify our selfish and hurtful actions;
remind us of the self-control that you require of us.

Silence

Jesus Christ entered our world to offer forgiveness and new life;
through him your sins are forgiven.
Thanks be to God. Amen.

Look out, you hypocrites!

Paraphrase of Matthew 23.13-36

Look out, you hypocrites!
You will know great trouble and distress. Why?
Do you not know that you lock people out of God's realm?
You know nothing of the joy of entering life and so you create
ridiculous rules that prevent others from growing closer to God.

Look out, you hypocrites!
You will know great trouble and distress. Why?
You use every means possible
and travel the world to make one single convert.
And then, what do you do?
You make the new convert even more rigid,
prejudiced and unloving than you are yourselves.
You teach them all of God's zeal and nothing of God's grace.
You labour your teaching of judgement
and skip lightly over any idea of mercy.
You place all your emphasis upon our distance from God,
our unworthiness, our fallen state.
You teach nothing about our being made in God's image,
our being precious children of God who will never be abandoned.

Beware, you unseeing guides!
You will know great trouble and distress. Why?
Your lack of insight teaches you the cost of everything
and the value of nothing.
That which is truly sacred,
that which is touched by God means nothing to you.

Beware, you hypocrites!
You will know great trouble and distress. Why?
Do you not know what God requires of you?
You wander around glowing with pride at your faithfulness and piety.
What little you give to God and to those in need
is like herbs and spices put on old food to disguise the smell of decay.
Mint, dill and cumin will flavour a meal or fragrance a room
but they are worth nothing whilst the poor go hungry.
You neglect that which weighs most heavily on God's heart –
the treatment of the poor, the vulnerable, the weak.
You ignore God's little ones and seek your own glory.
You fail to understand or exercise justice and mercy.
Look out, you hypocrites!
You will know great trouble and distress. Why?
You spend much of your time worrying about appearances.
You are like cups and plates that shine on the outside
but inside are foul, not safe for food or drink.
You give every impression of generosity and simple living
but inside you are greedy and self-indulgent.
You have no vision, no insight!
Do you not realize that when the inside of a person is right with God
the outside will shine with love?

Look out, you hypocrites!
You will know great trouble and distress. Why?
You are shiny tombs that on the outside look beautiful
but inside are full of the bones of the dead and all kinds of awful things.
The breath of life is stale within you
and you poison the air with the falseness of your teaching.
You give every appearance of obeying the laws of your creating,
but you practise nothing of what you preach.

Beware, you hypocrites!
You will know great trouble and distress. Why?
Because you decorate the graves of the righteous,
whilst dismissing the value of the living.
You hallow the dead, and want to share in their inheritance
claiming your greater wisdom would have prevented you
from slaying the prophets.
You would have chosen better,
yet you long to have lived in those golden days of prophecy.
Well, look out!
For these days will not be so different from the days gone by.
Your wisdom will not prevent you from brutally killing and flogging
the sages, scribes and prophets that I am sending you.
Some you will crucify and upon you will fall the blood of the righteous.
The spilt blood of the A-Z of the holy, from Abel to Zechariah,
will fall upon this very generation.

Intercessions

Gracious God,
hear us as we pray to you for your world and your people.
You have created a wonderful world, full of beauty
    and extravagance;
yet our world is damaged by human folly and greed.
We pray for those places that suffer environmental damage ...
    polluted places ... impoverished landscapes ...
    carelessly farmed and thoughtlessly wasted.

Silence

Grant us the courage and skills to undo the damage
    so foolishly wrought,
and the wisdom to be better stewards in the future.
Gracious God: **accept our prayers**.

At the table of your choosing sit people of every colour,
    experience and ability;
yet we choose to build barriers between people.
We pray for people who suffer the consequences of our
    prejudice ...
    victims of hate crimes ...
    victims of racism, sexism and homophobia ...
    people disabled by the thoughtlessness of others ....

Silence

Grant us the courage and skills to challenge injustice in all its forms
and the honesty to recognize the prejudice inside ourselves.
Gracious God: **accept our prayers**.

You have given human beings free will to choose a path that leads to life;
yet throughout the world people are threatened by the freedom of others.
We pray for people who are robbed of their basic human rights ...
> prisoners of conscience ...
> victims of torture and unlawful imprisonment ...
> children damaged by abuse and by exposure to war ....

Silence

Grant us the courage and skills to enable the release of captives,
and the love to help those whose wounds need healing.
Gracious God: **accept our prayers**.

We offer our prayers in the name of Jesus,
who welcomes all to share at his table of plenty and freedom. **Amen**.

On eagle's wings

Have you not known? Have you not heard the story
of God's creation from the birth of time?
Do you not understand the breadth of glory
displayed since earth's foundation long ago?
It's God's embrace that circles all creation
and we, though small, are held within God's care.
God's hands stretch out the heavens like a curtain
and build a precious home for all of us to share.

And do they know, the rulers and the powers,
how fragile is their hold on history's plan?
God's Spirit breathes upon them and they wither,
and like dry grass they fly before the storm.
It is God's realm that stands beyond comparing.
'Who is my equal?' asks the Holy One.
'Open your eyes to heaven that I'm sharing,
I know your name, and I will call you every one.'

Have you not known? Have you not heard the story,
so boldly told, of our eternal God?
Who since creation still has not grown weary
of humankind, embraced and held in love.
It is God's love that makes us fly like eagles,
renews our strength and will not let us fall.
So we shall run, no cause will make us feeble,
the faithful of all ages, caught up in God's call.

Tune: Londonderry Air

Growing
together

Solid lines
form firm foundations
and safe boundaries.
Broken lines
seem less secure
but allow beauty.
Colours compliment
and shades surprise
as the complex community
finds its glory
in the tension
of relationship.

Growing together

'No fears, no hopes, but one equal possession' is a state that John Donne looks forward to enjoying in the house of God. But what is 'one equal possession' and is it possible in anything but the purest of human love? Love is not lived in a holy vacuum but in the everyday practicalities and ups and downs of life.

Within all relationships the realities of who holds the power or has most to gain or lose will shift with time and circumstances. This is as true within ecumenical relationships as it is between friends and lovers. Recognizing the shifting ground of context and need is important within any relationship.

To grow together is to seek to be like God. The love of God is a creative space in which the beloved are allowed to grow, to learn, to live and to make choices. God's love is at its most dramatic and astonishing in that letting go of power that is the incarnation, life and death of Jesus.

The choices Jesus made created a space into which the totality of God's love could be poured and from which new life could spring. It is in that love that there are truly 'no fears, no hopes, but one equal possession'.

Letters between friends

Dear Ruth,

I see it – in frowning faces
I hear it – in whispered words
I feel it – in cold turned-away shoulders
Suspicion, hard as rock.

'She's fickle, that Orpah – comes and goes.'
'Ship slowly sinking? She'll be off with the rats.'
'Back she comes, but are we good enough this time?'

They love me but a gap has grown.
    I've grown, heaven help me.
    Things have changed.
    I've changed, heaven help us all.

It's hard, going back.
Was it right?

I love my people, the old ways, yet …

I miss you, Ruth.
        Love,

Orpah

Dear Orpah,

I see it – in frowning faces
I hear it – in whispered words
I feel it – in cold turned-away shoulders
Suspicion, hard as rock.

'Coming here with her strange ways.'
'Bewitching Boaz with her fancy foreign favours.'
'Mimicking our Yahweh yearning – is she sincere?'

They will love me, the gap is closing.
    I've grown closer, with heaven's help.
    Things are different here.
    I'm different too, with heaven's help.

It's been hard, going forward
But it was right.

I love my people, the new ways.

I miss you too, Orpah.
    Love,

Ruth

Prayer for a friend

My prayer is that God will diminish the distance between us.

My prayer is that our souls will communicate and know
    what it is to be connected with each other and creation.

My prayer is that such friendship as this will be of benefit to us
    but will bring no harm to others.

My prayer is that together we can laugh and cry,
    star-gaze and day-dream.

My prayer is that we will not sour our care for one another
    with jealousy or untruth
        but will allow truth and trust to guide our relationship.

My prayer is that we will remain friends
    in spite of distance or circumstance
        and that we will each help the other to grow
            and live life to the full.

My prayer is that I might help you to touch God and in doing so
    to fulfil the potential granted to you by divine wisdom.
                                        Amen.

You will be all that God intends

Future's misty horizon draws closer,
Clearer, bolder, more vivid with each dawn.
More exciting, scary, full of opportunity
    for your joy, for life in abundance.

Memories do not go but blend into future's
    beauty as God draws you towards
        the true you in all your glorious potential.
Walk boldly into that future place
    where each untold possibility will become
        your story.

(For Lorraine)

Keep singing

For a good friend who was a professional singer before becoming an Anglican priest

You have brought many songs into my life;
a song of love for life,
Wrought in the fire and pain of death,
    bereavement, rejection and conflict.
Yet finished in the fires of birth,
    passion, acceptance and reconciliation.
You have lived such a song of love.

You have brought many songs into my life;
a song of love for God,
Born in the excited questioning of youth,
    questioned, silenced and indoctrinated!
Yet developed in the excited questioning of adulthood,
    freed, feminist and fantastic!
You have lived such a song of love.

You have brought many songs into my life;
a song of love for this friend,
Composed in the community of change,
    late nights, long talks and painful honesty.
Yet arranged in the community now dispersed,
    parted, connected and loving still.
You have lived such a song of love.

You have brought many songs into my life;
a song of joy for women to be priested,
born in the barren wasteland of missed opportunities,
    injustice, rejection and despair.
Yet sung loudly in the rich diversity of new opportunities
    challenge, acceptance and loud celebration!
You have lived such a song of love.

Song of songs

Paraphrase of the woman's voice

I am black and beautiful.
Why should I be like one who is veiled?
I am a rose of Sharon, a lily of the valleys.

My beloved is mine and I am his.
Upon my bed at night I sought him, beloved of my soul.
    I sought him but found him not.
I rise and wander the city streets,
    seeking him whom my soul loves.

I found him, I held him and would not let him go
    until I brought him into my mother's house
        and into the chamber of she who bore me.

I slept, but my heart was awake.
I heard my beloved calling to me.
I yearned for him deep in my soul.
Naked and bathed, I arose to open to my beloved.
My fingers dripped with liquid myrrh upon the handles of the bolt.
I opened the door but my beloved had turned and gone.
    Down, down to his garden
        to the spice beds, to pasture his flock and gather lilies.

I am my beloved's and my beloved is mine.
I went down to the nut orchard
    to gaze at the blossoms,
    to see if the vines had budded
    and if the pomegranates were in bloom.
Before I was aware, my prince was beside me.

I am my beloved's and his desire is for me.
Come, let us go forth into the fields and lodge in the villages.
Let us go out early to see budding vines,
    grape blossoms
    and pomegranates in bloom.
There I will give you my love.

Hold me forever in your heart.
Death finds its equal in love and passion is as fierce as the grave.
Passion flares with the heat of a raging flame.
The seven seas cannot quench the flame of love;
    no flood can drown it.
Do not offer me the wealth of the ages for love,
    I will reply with contempt.

My vineyard, my very own, I will keep
    but you, my lover, may have the fruit.
Make haste, my beloved.
    Leap swift and sure-footed as the gazelle,
I am black and beautiful.

All of
me

You are with me as I wake.
As I plough my way through the mundane,
the ordinariness of everyday survival,
you provide a focal point,
a relief from the regular,
		dry dullness of me.

God has blessed me.
You are a gift, of great value.

In moments of stress
		you bring calm;
like a sunbeam, piercing the clouds.
In the tiring, trying things,
		you keep me sane.

You are like my favourite memories.
The Dales of my childhood,
		the colours of autumn at Brough.
I want to share with you the secret places
		where I spent childish days in muddy streams
		and pleasant fields,
		the places that made me who I am.

I want you to understand the life running through me.
I want you to know what I think, feel and see.
I want you to know my faith, family and friends.
I need you to understand me for all that I am.

I need to understand you,
to touch the depths,
		the hidden you.
I want to see more than your surface,
		hold more than your body.
I want you to feel as incomplete without me
		as I feel without you.

(For Sandy)

The Peace

Jesus said,
'I ask that they may all be one.
As you, Father, are in me and I am in you, may they also be in us,
so that the world may believe that you have sent me.'
May the peace of Christ bind us in unity.

Peace be with you:
And also with you.

Show us
the way

As we offer God our worship,
Spirit draw near.
As we meet in faith and friendship,
Spirit draw near.
Take us, shake us and remake us.
Guard us, guide us and provide us
with your gifts that have inspired us.
Spirit draw near.

Jesus' call our life is moulding
God's will be done.
Justice, peace and love upholding
God's will be done.
Preaching, teaching and revealing
truths that bear no more concealing.
Where love is there will be healing.
God's will be done.

We are pilgrims on a journey.
Show us the way.
Grant your children blessings many.
Show us the way.
You have called us to your service;
life abundant is your promise.
To new life in all its fullness
show us the way.

Tune: Ar hyd y nos

Challenges

Darkness closes in.
Vision dimmed by tears;
and fear's
noisy heartbeat
prevents all hearing.
Hands grasping,
breath gasping.
No more teaching,
no more preaching,
no more just being
who I have become.
Who have I become?
What more can I give?
Why should I live
with this decision?
What great mission
requires so great a price?

Challenges

There are times in life when all that we felt safe with seems to melt away. Long-held opinions and views about the world are no longer set in stone. The adolescent clarity about right and wrong is replaced by a thick cloud of unknowing and the map no longer makes sense.

The challenge of 'grey areas', complex moral and ethical decisions, can help us to reach a new horizon. We may not have one clear direction any longer but we are better equipped to enjoy the diversity of experiences on the journey. There are other times when our beliefs are as strong as ever; we have just lost the energy to keep going. This may be because we struggle alone or because we can see no progress despite our best efforts. It seems that the best thing to do is go with the flow and see where we are led.

The challenge Jesus faced at Gethsemane was something beyond our experience; we can only imagine the anguished questioning and the isolation. 'Enough faith' and 'Gethsemane' try to capture a sense of that struggle.

Not all challenges leave us despairing or facing our own private crucifixion. 'Sensing a call' focuses on how being called by God to serve in a new way involves asking lots of questions and can involve letting go of many things. Meeting the challenge can also be a new beginning, a radical departure bringing new life and opportunities previously undreamt of.

Longing for a Good Friday ending

As the crowd shouts 'Crucify her'
I stand, silent;
robbed of any word of defence.
My motivation for standing out
     forgotten, unimportant.

I stand, silent;
wishing I had never picked up this cup,
never thirsted for righteousness,
never hungered for justice.
The battle seems so old now
     and leaves me tired.

I stand, silent;
looking for something to lean on.
No longer wanting escape,
no longer finding excuses.
I feel so very old now
     and cannot go on.

I stand, silent;
sorting out the words in my mind,
which I can't articulate,
which I can't understand.
Nail me to your tree now
     and allow this to end.

Drowning or surviving?

Looking for a lifeline,
lifebelt,
lifetime
of not having to face this struggle.

Not again,
start again.
Need a gain,
just one victory.

Holding on,
moving on,
clinging on
to those long-held dreams.

Wandering,
wondering,
weaning myself
from needing your support.

Not another
Mothering Sunday

Where do the unwillingly childless find comfort
in the stories of Sarah, Hannah and Elizabeth?
Their faithfulness apparently rewarded
with the proof of God's favour.
Bearers in old age
of Yahweh's young prospects
for a future nation,
a privileged generation.
The long empty longing,
the sleepless nights
and disappointing mornings
ended for these foremothers
of faith.

What of those whose faithfulness
leaves only a bitter taste
and a sense of waste?
The old tales tell of punishment,
blaming women for failing
to bear fruit.

Of course, we don't believe that today?
Yet, in long Latin prose,
old men, barren and powerful
still declare
that women's lives
be measured
by their ability to be like
a particular teenage single mother.

In the wilderness

God who calls us on our journey,
as we remember Jesus' time in the wilderness,
help us to cast aside those things
that get in the way of hearing your word.
Help us to seek you in the places of bounteous beauty
and of barren bleakness.
Help us to seek you in the faces of friends
and in the smiles of strangers.
Help our devotion be made real in the actions of our lives.
When we have looked deep into our own hearts
and struggled with who we are,
send angels to minister to us and draw us out from our own wilderness
to fulfil our calling to serve you.
In Jesus' name.

Amen.

Jesus laments over Jerusalem

Jerusalem!
Jerusalem the place where
the prophets are killed,
the truth tellers stoned,
the peace bringers torn apart.

Jerusalem!
I long to be to you a mother hen caring for my brood.
I long to gather your children together.
I long to give you peace and bring you healing.

Jerusalem!
Will you not heed my invitation?
Must you continue to tear yourself apart?
Are you not willing to listen?

Jerusalem!
You will be left desolate.
I leave you now.
Even when you shout,
'Hosanna, blessed is the one who comes in the name of the Lord!'
your praise will soon fade to numbed silence
and your joy will make way for tears.

They have come so far.
    If only they knew
        how close we are to the end;
            how just beyond
                the dawn of their perception
                    lies the secret of salvation.

Enough faith?

                We have come so far.
                    If only you knew
                    how I have longed to drink
                    deep from the cup of obedience;
                    yet now there is no satisfaction
                    in the bitter dregs of an unanswered question.

        I have come so far.
        If only I knew.
        Is my faith enough
        to bear me on the bough
        of death's destruction
        and beyond to resurrection?

Gethsemane

All this effort,
is it worth it?
What difference my death?
What possible difference can it make in this world?
My enemies gather in the dark shadows,
I feel their antipathy, their anxious, excited anticipation,
I sense their incensed, self-righteous, unholy expectation.

All this effort,
is it worth it?
What difference my death?
What possible difference can it make in this world?
My friends sleep in the dark shadows,
I feel their confusion, their careful words and worried glances,
I sense their fear, their failing faith falling into despair.

All this effort,
is it worth it?
What difference my death?
What possible difference can it make in this world?
My God, are you there in the shadows?
I feel your prompting, parental prodding towards promise and duty,
I sense your pain, contained in this bitter cup you urge me to drink.

All this effort,
is it worth it?
What difference my death?
What possible difference can it make in this world?
Here I am, here, deep in the shadows.
I feel your strength, flowing as an offering through my fear,
I sense there will be more, I choose the cup, its contents and its cost.

Sensing
a call

Gracious God,
how can I serve you?
Where does my ministry lie?
There are so many jobs not done,
so many tasks that seem too large,
too difficult, too frightening for me.

What are my gifts, God?
What tools have you given me
that I might use to serve you?

Am I serving you now as you would wish?
Or do I have a long way to go?
Show me a sign in the midst of my confusion.
Put the writing on the wall.

Which of my experiences do you wish me to use?
Who amongst my friends should I ask for advice?
Do I make up excuses to avoid serving you?
Do I ignore the doors that you open?
Can I change anything?

I feel so weak, God.
Yet, I know that you will give me the gifts I need
to do your work.
Because you love me,
you will never ask too much of me.

Help me to hold fast to your promises
as I continue my journey with you.

Celebrations

Spread the cloth;
fetch the candles;
lay the table;
prepare the feast.

Feel the fluid folds of the fair linen.
Smell the yeasty, freshly baked bread.
See love's light reflected in each other's eyes.
Hear the liturgy of laughter and life's stories.
Taste the hearty wholesome wine
    and the crumbly comfort of the bread.

Bring all your senses to this table.
Bring all the busy-ness of your day.
Bring the jokes and silly stories;
Bring the wandering and the wondering.

Come and celebrate life-giving bread;
Come and celebrate good wine;
Come and celebrate living water;
Come and celebrate.
Come, all is ready.

Celebrations

Many of the times of worship in our lives are celebrations – the worship leader is often called the 'celebrant'. Celebrations are special times in our lives but as people of faith and hope we are called to celebrate God's presence in the world every day.

It is our sharing of bread and wine that most clearly 'celebrates' the mystery at the heart of faith. It is in the apparently everyday acts of eating and drinking, of sharing a meal with friends, that we mark most profoundly the union of the human and the divine. This 'sacramental celebration' is honoured by the church at particular times and in particular places and cared for by particular people. However, sacramental living – recognizing the presence of God in the everyday – is something all people of faith are called to.

The majority of items in this chapter are written for use as part of a celebration of Communion. The items throughout this book, however, are also about celebration – a celebration of sacramental living that recognizes that no part of our lives remains untouched by God.

Prayers of adoration and confession

For use at an annual celebration for the children baptized and blessed in a church

Gracious God,
we praise you for this day,
we offer you our worship, our adoration and our thanks.

Thank you for this wonderful world,
for all the beauty that surrounds us,
for the love we find in one another
and for the peace which comes from knowing you.

We think today of all the children who have been
baptized, blessed and welcomed here in this church
and praise you for their place in the universal,
worldwide Church of Jesus Christ.

We thank you for those who have helped the Christian nurture
of children and young people in the past
and those who continue to have special responsibility
for the care of little ones today.

We thank you for our own baptism,
for those who have cared for us
and encouraged us in faith and in maturity.
We praise you for those who helped us on our own journey of faith
and those who taught us that love is the most precious gift of all.

We confess that we have not always recognized the value of that gift
and we have taken for granted the riches of your love.
We know that we have hurt others,
let ourselves down and disappointed you.
We have not always kept our promises
and through cruel words, selfish actions, prejudice and fear,
we have dishonoured the image of Jesus in the world.

Loving God, we know that Jesus promises to forgive
those who are truly sorry. So in silence now we remember
before you those things we need to confess.

Silence

Thank you, Jesus, for forgiving us,
help us to do better in the future
and give us strength to do your will.
In your name we pray. Amen.

Celebrating journeys

I wish, living and loving God,
O ancient, eternal creator,
for a place in the wilderness,
that it may be my dwelling.

For the sound of birdsong,
that it may be my music;
for a clear pool,
that it may be my bathing place.

For a tree under which to sit,
that it may be my shelter;
for the stars above my head,
that the sky may be my cathedral.

There may I meet you, God of heaven,
and know that I am your child and you love me.

The Lord's Supper

Gathering

Welcome to this holy place,
and to this sacred time,
As we come together, one family, each with our part to play,
we remember that God is with us as host and guest:
>   listening to us and speaking to us
>   receiving from us and giving to us
>   intimately knowing us and unstintingly loving us.
So we offer, through our worship:
>   all that we have been,
>   all that we are
>   and all that in God we shall be.

Adoration

Mother God,
words cannot express our wonder at the beauty
and extravagance of all that you have made.
We adore you and offer you our worship.

The span of every human generation is too short
to describe the works of your hand.
We adore you and offer you our worship.

We find ourselves amazed at the depth
and breadth of your love for us, your children.
We adore you and offer you our worship.

The story of your saving love is miraculous and full of mystery.
We adore you and offer you our worship.

The generosity of your grace is shown in the life of your Son, Jesus Christ.
We adore you and offer you our worship.

The gentle dance of your Spirit moves through our lives
and brings us peace.
We adore you and offer you our worship.
Receive our prayers and be known to us in our worship.
In Christ's name. Amen.

Get everything ready

Luke 22.7-13

Get everything ready, it's almost time.
Prepare the place, the bread and the wine.
Follow the man carrying water,
carefully balancing that which gives life.

Get everything ready, it's almost time.
Prepare the place, the bread and the wine.
Go to the room that's ready upstairs,
all is laid out, plate, goblet and knife.

Get everything ready, it's almost time.
Prepare the place, the bread and the wine.
Let the feasting begin, the singing and sharing,
as we start preparing for the cost and the strife.

Affirmation

We believe in God,
prolific and passionate;
who parents creation
with extravagant love.

We believe in God,
holy and wholesome;
who nurtures her children
with patience and care.

We believe in God,
wise and willing;
who risks giving freedom
that we might choose love.

We believe in Jesus,
courageous and caring;
who lived among us
that we might know God.

We believe in Jesus,
healer and wounded;
who died among us
that we might have life.

We believe in Jesus,
risen and ascended;
who broke bread with us
that we might have hope.

We believe in God's Spirit
gentle and generous;
who giggles and dances
within our lives.

We believe in God's Spirit
fiery and forceful;
who challenges our apathy
and moves us to act.

We believe in God's Spirit
creative and captivating;
who calls us to be whole,
to be all that God intends.

Thanksgiving

God be with you:
And also with you.

Lift up your hearts:
We lift them up in praise.

It is good to worship God:
It is right to give our thanks.

Gracious God,
As your people, gathered in this place,
we offer our worship and thanksgiving.
Remembering that you created order out of chaos
and passionate life from sterile emptiness,
we praise you for all that you have made:
Blessed are you, Holy Creator.

Throughout human history
you have been active,
displaying your love for all that you have made.
You sent women and men of faith and wisdom
to tell your message of life and peace.
We praise you for your wisdom working in our world:
Blessed are you, Holy Spirit.

We failed to understand your message
and turned away from the blessings of your covenant promise.
You did not give us up but made yourself small
entering our world as a vulnerable child.
We praise you for the Word made flesh, dwelling among us:
Blessed are you, Holy Child of God.

We did not recognize Jesus as your child,
causing him to be put to death for our sake.
On the cross you gathered Jesus and all creation to yourself,
and three days later brought him back to life,
reconciling all that had been, all that is and all that ever shall be.

Remembering all these things,
we join together with those who love God, as we say:

Holy, holy, holy God,
gentle and strong,
heaven and earth are full of your glory.
Hosanna in the highest.

On the night before Jesus gave up his life,
he sat with his friends.
He took a loaf of bread, and when he had given thanks,
he broke it and gave it to them, saying,
'This is my body, it is given for you.
Do this to remember me.'

And he did the same with the cup after supper, saying,
'This is my blood of the new covenant,
poured out for all for the forgiveness of sins.
Do this to remember me.'

Christ has died.
Christ is risen.
Christ will come again.

So in remembrance of Jesus' self-giving love,
we offer our sacrifice of praise and thanksgiving,
asking you to accept these your gifts,
this bread and this wine.

Send your Holy Spirit upon us that we might be one
and upon these gifts that they might be for us
the body and blood of Jesus Christ.

Broaden our vision,
strengthen our faith,
welcome us and all people into the circle of your love.

To you, loving God,
through your Son, Jesus Christ,
in the unity of the Spirit,
be all honour and glory
now and for ever.
Amen.

Take this cup

Leader: 'Take this cup and hide it in my brother's bag of grain.'
A wine cup, grain to make bread.

All: **Part of God's plan to show love is not dead.**

Leader: 'Take this cup, and this bread and remember.'
A wine cup, a plate full of bread.

All: **Part of God's plan to show love is not dead.**

Leader: 'Take this cup, but let it be according to your will.'
A wine cup, a night filled with dread.

All: **Part of God's plan to show love is not dead.**

Leader: 'Take this cup, overflowing with abundant life.'
A wine cup; you, our body's risen head.

All: **You are God's plan to show love is not dead.**

Leader: We take this cup, we break your body and we remember.
A wine cup, a plate for the bread.

All: **We are God's plan to show love is not dead.**

Re – membering

Lilith, Hagar and Vashti
dis-membered by history's amnesia, rightly cry:
'How long, O God? Will you forget me forever?'

In our taking, thanking, breaking and sharing,
Let us re - member them.

Lydia, Junia and Prisca
dis-membered by patriarchy's power, rightly cry:
'How long, O God? Will you forget me forever?'

In our taking, thanking, breaking and sharing,
Let us re - member them.

Nameless saints, holy anonymous heroines
dis-membered by the need of the powerful to maintain
        the status quo, rightly cry:
'How long, O God? Will you forget me forever?'

In our taking, thanking, breaking and sharing,
Let us re - member them.

Women struggling to stay in the Church
and those who take the struggle elsewhere
dis-membered by exclusive patterns of worship
        and community, rightly cry:
'How long, O God? Will you forget us forever?'

In our taking, thanking, breaking and sharing,
We re - member ourselves.

Taste the bread!

John 6.50-51   (For two voices, last stanza together)

Taste the bread!

> *What bread?*
> *Brown, white, smooth, granary?*
> *Will it melt in my mouth*
> *or be crusty against my teeth?*

Don't ask so many questions;
taste the bread!

> *Why me?*
> *When many are without bread,*
> *or rice, or meat, or vegetables.*
> *How can I eat?*

This bread is for all;
taste the bread!

> *Where should I eat?*
> *In church, chapel, cathedral,*
> *in homes, the street, in community?*
> *Where should I eat?*

This bread is in all places;
taste the bread!

This bread that is Jesus Christ, broken, blessed,
offered freely, is the bread of life.
It is the living bread of heaven.

This living bread brings eternal life.
It is not limited to time, place, person or situation.
It is God given.

> **Taste the bread!**
> **The living bread that comes from heaven.**
> **Taste the bread!**
> **The bread that Christ gives for the life of the world.**
> **Taste the bread!**
> **And know that you have life within you.**

All will
be well

Red arrow, forcing up
through the energy draining
life staining
complex chemistry
of disease.
A 'totaliser' of an arrow
counting countless lives lost.
Or do you represent hope,
breaking through the mass of despair,
breaking the continuum of infection?
Pinks and purples
suggest death and mourning,
or healing and hope.
Do your colours point to God
or to the gods we make
of companies that choose
who to heal
and who to profit from?

All will be well

Each generation of human history has seen its plagues. Relentless diseases raging out of hand until a change of circumstance or a medical breakthrough has offered salvation. There has always been a gap between the survival rates of the rich and poor but until recent history this gap has been quite small. Human beings no longer understand death through disease as God's will. We know that doctors and advances in medical science will prolong our lives. The gap in the survival rates between those who can afford drugs and those who cannot is enormous. HIV has shown the difference between the haves and the have-nots in the cruellest of ways.

How do we make sense of a God of love who became a human healer, in the face of HIV and of a world where diseases long preventable and curable continue to kill millions? Do we agree with the 'Cynics' of old that these things are a cycle in which history is destined to repeat itself or do we choose to continue to hope in the face of despair?

The God I believe in at the depths of my being is a God who longs for wholeness and healing for all people. Those of us who share this hope cannot ignore our responsibility to work for and call for change in our world. There is no soft or comfortable option; we are called to make a difference – through our prayers, through our protests and through our actions. We do not know how all will be well, but like Julian of Norwich we do know that 'all manner of things will be well'.

For the forgiveness of sins

Blood marked the doors of those who sought God's mercy
but the cries of Egypt's mothers still ring in history's ears.
This is my blood poured out for you for the forgiveness of sins.

Bloodshed was deemed to be a sign of God's chosen ones
as a wandering people waged war and claimed Yahweh's blessing.
This is my blood poured out for you for the forgiveness of sins.

A powerful king slaughtered vulnerable children
and Rachel's daughters wept as blood filled the streets.
This is my blood poured out for you for the forgiveness of sins.

A woman who bled for long years, bearing exclusion
was made whole by passing on her 'uncleanness'.
This is my blood poured out for you for the forgiveness of sins.

Women who shed blood as part of the pattern of co-creation
have been declared unclean by generations of barren priestly men.
This is my blood poured out for you for the forgiveness of sins.

Bleeding has always been a risky business,
life's ebb and flow marked in heartbeat's rhythm.
This is my blood poured out for you for the forgiveness of sins.

Now three generations of Africa's children die
as blood continues to carry the possibility of life and death.
This is my blood poured out for you for the forgiveness of sins.

HIV marks the blood of millions
as positive becomes negative in a deadly fight against time.
This is my blood poured out for you for the forgiveness of sins.

Does this new passing of the angel of death
change anything about our understanding of Christ's words?
This is my blood poured out for you for the forgiveness of sins.

Whose blood is being poured now and who is unclean?
Whose sins are being forgiven in a global market for life?
This is my blood poured out for you for the forgiveness of sins.

In Simon's house at Bethany

They used to call him 'Leper', my friend Simon. He did have some sort of rash, poor guy. It used to drive him crazy, scratching until he made himself bleed. But it wasn't like real leprosy; he could still feel. He felt all the priests' attempts at a cure, felt the cold look of dismissal; felt the painful rejection from the holy places and the fearful, pitying looks of his family and friends.

I liked Simon, he was kind and brave, he didn't make a fuss and he kept his sense of humour. The holy ones did not accept me, either, I'm not sure why. They've always had a low opinion of women and I'm a bit too outspoken for them. I think they believe the rumours about me. That's the religious ones for you – always ready to believe the worst and to indulge in gossip.

So, sometimes I would take some ointment to Simon, something soothing, nothing posh mind, or expensive. Just some rubbing oil I'd bought at the market. I don't know if it helped but Simon was always grateful. I guess it was the fact that someone would spend time in the same room as him despite the rulings of the holy Joes!

Then things got better for Simon. Jesus walked into our little town. He had a calm look in his eyes. Those eyes that could see deep into the very heart of you! Often a smile played close to his lips and he had a laugh as deep as the sea at Galilee. He had a kindness about him that touched you at the very core. The only time I heard him say unkind things was about the hypocrisy of them lot up at the Temple. You should have heard him then!

Jesus went to Simon's house, walked straight in and sat down. Simon grinned; he seemed to know instinctively that this man was special. He made some drinks and talked with Jesus. Simon did not ask Jesus to cure him, didn't even talk about his skin problem. They talked about prayer and what mattered to God and got really excited when they realized how many of their ideas were the same. You know how it is when you make a new friend and the stories and ideas flow like wine at a wedding! After a while there was a comfortable silence. Jesus looked for a long time at Simon with a look so full of love you could feel its warmth all around the house. In that look was a question and Simon nodded his answer. From his lips spilled the words, 'Yes, Lord, I do want to be whole, to be well, to live life in all its fullness. I want to know you and to be one with God.' Jesus smiled, touched Simon's face and said, 'All is well.'

That was it! No fancy rituals, no shouting, singing, prancing about or long ghastly sermons. Simon was well – all was well. I have never known peace like there was in that place. In that moment my heart swelled and I knew that I loved Jesus with every fibre of my being.

Jesus came to Bethany a few times after that and would stay at Simon's house. I loved his visits, we all did. Not the super-righteous ones from the synagogue – they sensed competition, they were jealous that Jesus was so popular. I was delighted when Jesus came, I could sit and listen to his teaching all day and night. He didn't always teach, sometimes he told jokes and he would always laugh at the jokes the old men told. He laughed loudest at old Ben's jokes, which was kind because Ben always messed up the punch-line!

We would sing songs and Jesus would encourage the children to join in. And always there was a sense of love and peace and joy. Mind you, the last couple of visits the conversation turned to darker matters. Jesus started to talk about being killed. I didn't want to believe him but I knew that the religious elite had it in for him. I began to feel afraid for him, tried to tell him to be careful. He would look at me with those penetrating eyes and tell me not to fear and that whatever happened all would be well.

One day I was in the market and the stall where I used to get Simon's ointment had some new jars. Really beautiful colours, they were. One caught my eye – it was a deep purple, a royal colour, the colour of wealth and death. I kept coming back to it and in the end I asked the stall-keeper how much. Well, I nearly collapsed on the spot! It contained nard, dead expensive at the best of times but this was a king's ransom. I walked away; it was too rich for *my* pocket.

I couldn't get that jar out of my head – it was so beautiful. I have never seen such an exquisite shape and such a deep, soulful purple. I went back to the stall a few days later and the nard was still there. I suggested a low price and got the answer I expected but we bartered and finally got to a figure I could afford. I had a bit of an argument inside my head – you know, 'What do you want that for? No one's died – I can't believe you'd spend your life savings on that, have you lost your senses?'

I knew, though. I knew that I was going to keep it for Jesus. If he really was going to die then he would have the best embalming ever, and I would give him a gift in death that my people's traditions prevented me giving him in life. Mind you, that's not quite what happened.

Jesus came to Simon's house again. It was just before the Passover and rumour had it that the chief priests were at fever pitch over Jesus and what he had been teaching.

He looked tired, an air of sadness seemed to settle over the house and the smile no longer played on his lips. Jesus looked over at me and, as his eyes met mine, I felt my heart go out to him. This man who had done so much for Simon, for my friends and for me, needed help. I leapt up, ran to my house across the square and pulled the rugs and cups from the lid of the chest where I had stored my precious jar. 'Don't let him leave, God. Please still be there when I get back.'

I could feel panic rising in me as my fingers lifted the heavy wooden lid. My heart raced as my hands wrapped themselves round the perfect smoothness of the container and I lifted it out. I ran back to Simon's, more slowly now for fear of dropping my valuable gift. I went through the door. 'Still here, he's still here!' My heart almost burst with joy.

I pushed past his friends, those who were always with him, ignoring their grunts of displeasure and censure. I knelt down in front of Jesus and banged the jar on the hard floor. It cracked, and two perfect halves of purple clay opened in my hands. The smell, oh, the smell! It was intoxicating, a perfume so sweet it seemed to smell of the very flowers of heaven. Yet it was not a sickly smell, there was something of musk and earthiness and human love about this ointment. The rushing stopped, my breathing steadied and, in what seemed like slow motion, I stood. I raised the pieces of the jar above his head and allowed the oil to pour over his hair, his neck, his forehead, his shoulders. It seemed to pour on and on, flowing with love and healing and life. Inside myself I felt anointed, liberated, healed and loved, loved beyond all telling.

Jesus sat very still. He received the gift, in all its messiness and all its glory, he accepted it. Jesus received me, accepted me in all my messiness and all my glory. As the last of the ointment dripped like honey from the broken jar, I sank to my knees at his feet. I wept, oh, how I wept. I wept for all the love I had finally understood and for all the love I had never experienced. I wept for Jesus in my knowledge that his journey would soon become one travelled in the dark. I wept with the knowledge that this man was truly God's child and that his presence brought God into my world.

Jesus rubbed the ointment into his skin and hair, as his disciples muttered and grumbled about waste and money and the poor. Jesus put his hand under my chin and lifted my face up to him. Looking me in the eye he answered them, 'She has done something so beautiful for me. I will not always be with you and she has understood this. She has, in her love, anointed my body for burial. Do you not realize that whenever my story is told, she will be remembered for this gift of love?'

One of his friends left in something of a temper and a cold shadow fell upon the house, but Jesus did not seem afraid. Later, when he left for Jerusalem he looked at me for the last time, his eyes smiling, and said, 'All will be well.'

Intercessions

For this world in its need
   its need of peace
   its need of healing
   its need of love
Holy God, we pray.

For the nations in their need
   their need of peace
   their need of healing
   their need of love
Holy God, we pray.

For the body of Christ in its need
   its need of peace
   its need of healing
   its need of love
Holy God, we pray.

For your people in their need
   their need of peace
   their need of healing
   their need of love
Holy God, we pray.

For *this town* in its need
   its need of peace
   its need of healing
   its need of love
Holy God, we pray.

For our faith community in its need
   its need of peace
   its need of healing
   its need of love
Holy God, we pray.

For ourselves in our need
   our need of peace
   our need of healing
   our need of love
Holy God, we pray.

In the name of Christ. Amen.

In this time
of change

God of grace and power
    grant me peace in this time of change;
    grant me the wisdom to get the best out of each day;
    grant me love beyond measure,
        that I can return to others a portion of the love
          they have shown to me.

Protect those I love,
    remind me each day that I am your child
      and precious in your sight.

Hold me and shield me,
    bring me wholeness and strength,
      and grant me the knowledge that in you
        all will be well.
          Amen.
            (For Jim and Marian)

With sighs too deep for words

Prayer based on Romans 8.26-39

Listening God,
hear our silence and our fear of praying:
we worry that we will use the wrong words;
we cannot find words that begin to express how we feel;
we feel too small when faced with your greatness.
So hear our silence
and send your Spirit to pray for us with sighs too deep for words.

Silence

Loving God,
we know that all things work together for good for those who love you;
yet we forget the extent of your love.
You are for us! Who can be against us?
Why do we worry, is our faith so weak?
Remind us again that you did not withhold your own Son
but gave him up for all – even us.

Silence

Living God,
nothing in all creation can separate any of us
from your love in Christ Jesus.
Nothing – not a thing.
We turn away from even small problems,
we hate to be uncomfortable or inconvenienced;
we give in so easily.
Help us to believe the promise of your abiding,
eternal love which is present through death, through life,
through past, present and future.
Grant us the gift of faith which allows us to be truly 'faith-full',
to be effective disciples and willing storytellers,
proclaiming the gospel of Christ in whose name we pray. Amen.

Meditation

Clashing, harsh sounds crowd our everyday lives.
Traffic's noise. The hammering sounds of construction and demolition.
The shouting of angry voices. Constant demanding calls of other people.
The phone rings, shattering even one moment of quiet.

We long for silence.
We yearn for space amid the chaos.
We hope for an end to the cacophony.

Silence descends
in sleeping
in waiting
in watching for the dawn.
But there is still no peace.

Our minds are noisy with doubts.
We hear old conversations replayed in our heads.
Our mixed, confused, inner secrets tumble over each other in our minds.
In silence we are confronted with ourselves.
What will bring us peace?

King Saul's anguished spirit was soothed by music.
There is a space in the balm of soft sounds.
There is truth in harmony and melody.
If we cannot bear silence we may find ease in music.

Our own personal madness,
our own frightened insanity and
our own fear of facing up to ourselves
are as important as our sanity.
In these places our reliance on God is most real.

God is there in the angry, clashing noise.
God is speaking in the silence, waiting to be heard.
And God is moving in the music,
dancing an eternal dance of healing and love.

Now we put aside the noise,
empty ourselves of our fear of silence
and rest in the arms of our creator.

God who speaks in silence

God who spoke to Elijah in sheer silence
speak to us now.
Help us to be quiet enough to hear the voiceless.
Help us to listen to the excluded, the stranger, and the unexpected.
Open our ears and hearts to your word.

God who brought Elijah out of hiding
call to us now.
Confront us with the task you have for us.
Challenge us with uncomfortable truths.
Turn our comfort into action.

God who spoke to Mary through an angel
speak to us now.
Help us to be bearers of your word.
Help us to face a hostile world with courage.
Open our lives to the possibility of new life within us.

God who brought Jairus' daughter out of death
call to us now.
Grant us new life transformed by your love.
Give us new opportunities to serve you.
Turn our dis-ease into healing love.

Take our noise and quieten us.
Take our silence and hear us.
Take our injured voices and heal us,
that we may shout for you,
listen to you and work for you.
In the name of Jesus Christ.

Amen.

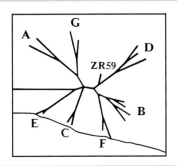

St GREGORY

Wisdom's gift

You seem young for a saint
captured in stained glass.
Do your wide eyes
take in the hues
that surround you?
The reds of danger and power
and the searing white of holiness
make a halo that seems
more protection than crown.
Yet wisdom descends,
hovers
moves over
the symmetry of your existence.
Like age, experience
and journeyed, dusty feet;
there is a price to wisdom.
It is rarely paid by the young
and often disregarded by the old.

Wisdom's gift

It is a challenge for someone who is not yet 40 to reflect upon the experience of old age. In churches where the newly retired are the young movers and shakers, the ideas of old and young take on new meaning. This chapter is a pause for observation, looking at the experience of others as they face the challenge of ageing. It is also a celebration of the wisdom and insight that can only come with experience.

Anyone who has spent time with people in nursing homes or geriatric wards cannot fail to be struck by the fascinating life stories of so many elderly people. It is all too easy to see 'another little old lady' with silver hair, elusive dentures and an even more elusive short-term memory. It takes a little more effort to learn about her as the young woman who drove munitions trucks in the Second World War and went on to be Finance Director of a local company. Attentive listening can reveal how someone you have only known as a carer for her husband was a systems analyst at a multinational corporation, or how the busy Rotarian church steward had helped develop radar technology.

The gift of time can be a feature of later years and a willingness to use what time we have for God's purposes is recognized in the prayer of confession in this chapter. The gift of grandchildren is also celebrated.

Wisdom does not always come through our own experiences – it is often a gift which comes through listening to the stories of others. It also comes through our willingness to listen to God through contemplation and through meditation on God's word. Learning to stop, to slow down and to listen will help us to grow as we allow God's Spirit of Wisdom to dwell in us.

What do you see?

When you look at me, what do you see?
An old lady in a dress you would not be seen dead in,
or a young girl dressed ready to meet her soldier boy?

When you look at me, what do you see?
A lonely widow with arthritic joints,
or a woman on her wedding night, supple and gifted?

When you look at me, what do you see?
A retired woman living long, empty days,
or a senior surgeon, leading her team?

When you look at me, what do you see?
A holier-than-thou woman with a pious look,
or an accomplished preacher with good news to share?

When you look at me, what do you see?
Someone with nothing left to look forward to,
or a person with the time and energy to enjoy life?

When you look at me, what do you see?
Do you see me, as I am and have been,
or do you see yourself and fear how things might be?

Confession

God of all time,
Forgive me when I waste precious time,
worrying or busying myself with pointless jobs.
Forgive me that I am so skilled in the art of procrastination.
Forgive me when I use activity to stop me spending time with you.
Forgive me when I am distracted from your purposes for my life
and for the lives of others.

Help me to make the most of the time available to me.
Help me not to keep waiting until 'the right time',
    putting off things that matter.
Help me to celebrate each day and each moment as a gift from you.

Thank you for forgiving me and for all your blessings.
In Christ's name.

Amen.

Thanksgiving for grandchildren

Creator God, I praise you,
I thank you for my grandchildren.

Thank you for their energy and noise;
for their enthusiasm and the love they generously give;
and for the frog that they brought in from the garden today.

Thank you for the muddy footprints and the toys everywhere;
for the gallery of finger-paintings and sticker pictures in my kitchen.

Thank you for the chance to read them bedtime stories
and to tuck them in with a lullaby.

Thank you for their songs and laughter that fill my house.
Oh yes, and thank you that they go back home tomorrow!

Amen.

Really listen

To listen to another person,
really listen;
not just hearing words
but what lies behind them.
To listen like that
is to make the other person important.

When we really listen,
hearing the pain or joy,
hearing the loneliness or confidence
    of the other person,
then we are giving something to them.

We are truly putting our neighbour before our self.
We are saying,
    'You are important to me.
    You matter and what you have to say matters.'

In the moments when you listen to someone else
you are no longer putting yourself first,
you stop being at the centre of the universe.

The more people learn to really listen to each other
the more peaceful the world will be
the closer we will be to living in God's will.

When we stop shouting,
when our voices and confusions are stilled,
when we no longer make our own opinion law
	and other people's folly,
then into the silence that follows
will come music and birdsong
and perhaps even the sound of trees growing.

And quietly, lovingly,
almost silently,
God's voice will be heard, saying,
'At last you have allowed me to exist.
At last you can hear my voice.
At long last, my child, you have learnt to love me.'

Meditation on Mark 12.28-34

God, our God, is one.
Just one God, is one enough?
There are so many things I want to worship:
>   comfort
>   safety
>   wealth
but God, one God,
you make me uncomfortable
you are unsafe
you make a mockery of the wealth I desire.

God, our God, is one.
Just one God, is one enough?
There are so many things I want to worship:
>   love that comes easily
>   the idea of love
>   love that meets my needs
but God, one God,
your love is not easy
your love is more than an idea
your love involves meeting the needs of others.

God, our God, is one.
How do I love you with all my heart,
when so many other things demand my care?
How do I love you with all my soul,
when I don't even understand what my soul is?
How do I love you with all my mind,
when I can't concentrate on one thing for more than a minute?
How do I love you with all my strength,
when I am so tired, so weak, so worn-out?
How can I love my neighbour
when I have never learned to love myself?

Can it really be that it is enough to begin?
That by just asking these questions I am somehow nearer God?
Can it really be that you, God, our God, one God
are there in the questions as well as the answers?
Can it really be that you, God, our God, one God
love me and my friends enough to make room for us in your embrace?
If it is so God, our God, one God, you are more than enough.

Uncomfortable
grace

Generous God,
it is very comforting to know that despite
all my weaknesses and all my strengths,
you love me and offer me as much as those I hold in high esteem.
No more and no less.
Such is grace.

Generous God,
it is less comforting to know that all those people I resent; I fear;
I judge to be racist, sexist, homophobic and unworthy,
are offered the same love.
No more and no less.
Such is grace.

Squaring
the circle

Durham Cathedral

The cathedral builders of old understood the secret,
    using codes and structures that told of God made human
        and order made from chaos.

The world, represented by squares,
    apparently irreconcilable to an eternal God drawn in circular form.

In columns, walls and soaring towers
    the human world connects with the divine.
No Babel tower, no idolatrous endeavour pointing to human glory.
There is a subtle, more sophisticated theology in this place.
The visible points to the invisible.
The tangible hints at the intangible.
The temporal gives way to the eternal.

The girth of great columns equals their height,
    if we could open them out they would be square.
Here, in the hidden, centuries old design
    is a message for those who can see.
We can square the circle,
    God and creation are reconciled.

The four corners of the earth meet
    in an eternal dance that is moved by God's own music.
The everlasting God embraces the things that human beings know
    and leads us to knowledge beyond our imagining.

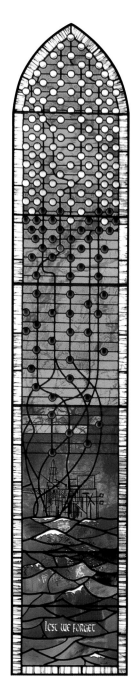

A glimpse of the

horizon beyond

lest we forget

Remember Bhopal, Chernobyl, Dunblane.
Remember Ethiopia, Hillsborough, Lockerbie.
Remember Piper Alpha, Soho, Palestine.
Remember the points on the map,
the geography of grief
the legacy of loss
the places of passion.
Innocuous places made infamous,
sacred places desecrated,
re-sanctified by tears,
made memorials by minds striving to remember.

A glimpse of the horizon beyond

The landscape of loss is made up of personal, national and corporate grief. Whatever the circumstances of a particular death, private and unnoticed by the world, or public and surrounded by a media frenzy, common themes emerge. Shock, denial, anger and grief combine with the need to make sense of events and the need to mark the occasion of loss.

When a specific location is a focus for grief this can become a place of memory. The Kop at Anfield was not the place in which tragedy occurred but it had represented a sacred place to those who died at Hillsborough and has become a place of memorial for those who lost loved ones. Few will forget the thousands of flowers in Kensington Gardens following the death of Diana, Princess of Wales. It is no longer unusual to see flowers laid at the sites of fatal road accidents. Memorials matter to people.

The Piper Alpha Memorial Window provides a focus for remembrance and, for those among the bereaved who had no physical remains to bury or scatter, a physical location to connect with loved ones. The window conveys a sense of hope, of life continuing beyond death. Each symbol of a life lost rises and becomes part of creation in a new and liberated way.

Words can also provide a focus for memory and an acknowledgement of our deepest emotions, fears and hopes. Platitudes are not enough in the face of the most extreme experiences of life. The prayers we offer at times of great loss need honesty that honours those who have died and creates space for our true feelings.

The prayers and poems in this chapter do not attempt to protect God from the anger and dismay of the bereaved but acknowledge God's presence in the mess and pain of loss. The classic stages of bereavement can be found in the writing of this chapter but not in a linear progression. Each day for those who grieve might contain any number of emotions. There are those days when you come up for air and realize at the end of the day that you have hardly thought about your loss. Yet there are also days, even years later, when the pain is as sharp as the first time you heard the news that changed your world for ever.

Grief is a thief

Grief is a thief;
    stealing
        the air from my lungs,
        the energy from my muscles,
        the desire from my appetite
           for food or love.

Grief is a thief;
    stealing
        sensation
        satisfaction
        sanctification
           and I am wholly undone.

Grief is a flash flood;
    outpouring
        instant pain,
        illogically triggered,
        immutable
           it will not be gainsaid.

Grief is a flat, empty landscape;
    it becomes
        absence
        aching nothingness
        apathy
           that scorns sympathy.

Grief is isolating;
    it is disconnection
        from the other
        from the self
        from the God
           who should be here.

Grief is a dull weight
    and a dull wait
        for change
        for relief
        for a way
           of living with new reality.

Grief

God,
it is so hard to connect with you when grief overwhelms me.
I am isolated from those around me
    and I do not even want to connect with them or you.
Hold me, even though I cannot feel you.
Be with me, even though I do not recognize your presence.
Trace the shape of my grief and contain it,
    that I can let it go,
        safe in the knowledge you will not reduce,
            belittle or betray this part of who I am.
                                        Amen.

Shock

No! No, God,
It isn't true – make it not true.
Let it all be a dreadful mistake.
I don't know what to do.
Help me, God,
help me to know:
    should I sit down or stand up?
    who should I call?
I can't think,
I can't get words out,
    how do I get through this?
Help me.
    Help me put one foot in front of the other.
    Help me to breathe one breath at a time.
    Help me to get through this.

Anger

I'm so angry.
I never expected life to be fair but this is beyond unfair.
It is cruel and I cannot understand.
The rage within me burns up all my energy
    and when I am fully consumed
        all that remains is a dull, empty ache.
All those sermons, all those times when I've heard or said
    that life's not simple and that God doesn't 'make' bad things happen
        – all so empty now.
I want a simple God who interferes,
    who helps the good and innocent and punishes the bad and guilty.
I'm angry because such belief is not mine – mine is complicated
    by my mind and my experience,
    by my theology and my spirituality.
I want to shout and scream and cry because my own need to move on
    betrays my need to stay with the trauma and pain.

God, accept my anger.
I do not believe it is wrong to feel this way.
Hold my anger,
    be angry alongside me.
You know anger;
you know through your own Son
    what it means to burn with desire for change,
        for life to come from death.
Accept my anger, hold it and honour it
    and, in doing so, accept, hold and honour me,
        your child.
                        Amen

Denial

God, could you believe what we did to your Son?

Did you shout 'No!' until all creation rang with thunder
     and your grief split the sky with lightning?

You denied death and your denial brought about life.
Why does my denial of my beloved's death just seem
     to bring more death?
I turn away from truth and seek sanctuary in pretence.
I turn away from life and bury myself behind walls
     of courage and false cheerfulness.
I turn away from you, the real you,
     and hide behind comfortable religion and pious cant.

When I deny others the reality of my grief,
     let them see through my pretence and hold me.
When I deny myself the truth of my emptiness,
     fill me with love and a calm peace.
When I deny you and replace you with empty ritual,
     become real again to me.
Constant God, help me to know that you will never deny me.
                                                  Amen.

A prayer for those asked to 'just be here'

God, who is always here,
help me to be in this place.

Help me to be calm and to listen.
Help me to put others' needs before my own.
Help me not to pretend I have answers
    or even that I know all the questions.

Help me to know when to offer an embrace
    and when to hold back.

Help me to create space for others to be here too.
Help me to know when to leave and when to return.
Help me to find the peace that only you can give.
    In Jesus' name.   Amen.

Prayer with the dying

Loving God,
remove from us all fear.

Remind us again of your promise
    of eternal life.
Help *N* to know that you prepare
    a place for *her/him*
    and that your love is constant
    in life and in death.
Grant strength and courage to *N*'s family and friends;
    and give to all your children
    the joy that your peace brings.
In Christ's name we pray.

                                 Amen.

At the scattering
of ashes

Loving God,
we trust your infinite love and tender mercy;
we rest our pain and fear in you.

Loving God,
it is time for parting
but we find it hard to end what has been so good.

Loving God,
you have known the pain of loss
and we share our hurt with you now.

We offer *N* to you.
This place was precious to *her/him*,
as *N* was precious to us.

We thank you for *her/his* life,
for our memories of *N*
and for the love we have shared between us.

We cast (place) *N* into the safe embrace of your loving arms,
holding and protecting *her/him* until the time
you draw all creation to yourself and we are reunited in love.
Your creating love will make all things new,
through Jesus Christ we pray. Amen.

Prayer for one who has chosen to take *her/his* own life

Compassionate God,
we gather in this place to give thanks for the life of *N*.
As we remember *him/her* and all *he/she* meant to us,
grant us the grace to remember times of joy and hope.

As we struggle to understand the choices that *N* has made,
grant us the courage to remember times of pain and fear.

As we confront our feelings of guilt and anger,
grant us the forgiveness promised by Jesus our Saviour.

As we continue our journey through grief and sadness,
grant us the healing and strength of the presence of your Spirit,
through Christ, our Lord. Amen.

For Lucy,
born still

A change, a fluttering, a sense of new beginning
    announced your conception
        and your journey began.

A growing, an unfolding, a sense of future hope
    marked your development
        and your journey continued.

A knowing, a waiting, a sense of looking forward
    marked your loving
        and your journey continued.

A fear, a cold grip on the heart, a sense of deep despair
    marked your dying
        yet your journey continued.

A struggle, a courageous woman, a loving man
    marked your birthing
        and your journey continued.

An emptiness, a longing, a sense of united grief
    marks your leaving
        yet you journey on …
            taking your light into God's house.

Lucy, our bringer of light,
    you have illuminated our lives,
we let you go, our world now darker.

When we think of you, remind us that to God
    the darkness and the light
        are both the same and hold no fear.

 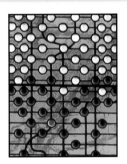

Making the colours sing

Wounded healer,
you reach for bread and wine
and in this act of blessing,
breaking and sharing,
your identity is made known.
Your vulnerable love is shown
as your body is broken again
and again,
in countless acts of cruel carelessness.
You defeat death again
in every act of selfless love.
You ascend again
in every human being who knows the
glory of being fully alive.
Your work continues
as the Spirit moves beyond Pentecost
and points all creation to a future
reconciled with God.

Making the colours sing

A number of films about the life of Jesus finish at the point of his death. Other approaches to the events of Easter Sunday and beyond can leave us with the idea that 'they all lived happily after. THE END'. A more thoughtful reading of the Bible text does not allow for either approach.

The followers of Jesus were in disarray after the events of Good Friday and their sense of loss was not overcome by any number of resurrection appearances. Ascension and Pentecost marked distinct stages in the story, yet the disciples' feelings of confusion did not completely end with the arrival of God's Spirit. In this we find hope. We know about God's promises of eternal life and of a time when all creation will be restored. Yet we do not always live as people of hope.

We can feel guilty if we are not certain about life after death, or wonder why suffering continues in our world. The idea that Christ's wounds were visible following the resurrection points to God's involvement in the broken messiness of real life. This last chapter contains items that reflect on resurrection, ascension and Pentecost, and on the idea of Christ as our 'Great High Priest', and ends with a number of blessings.

Blessings are more than a tidy way of ending a time of worship – or a book! They are an expression of love between those being blessed, the one proclaiming the blessing, and God who blesses. Blessings give permission for rest but also acknowledge that the journey continues, that there is more to say and more to do. The resting, the saying and the doing all take place within the context of God's love. May you journey well.

Don't tell me 'time's a healer'

(Two voices – Mary and a disciple)

Don't go to the garden, Mary; it's too soon, give it time.
There's nothing you can do, Mary, your broken heart will heal.

> *I must go, don't tell me 'time's a healer'.*
> *Eternity's not long enough to take this pain away.*

Don't go to the garden, Mary, it's too dangerous, stay safe hiding here.
There's nothing you can do, Mary, don't risk us all.

> *I must go – my safety's not important and neither is yours.*
> *He gave up everything, choosing no sanctuary or refuge.*

Don't go to the garden, Mary, you're hysterical.
There's nothing you can do, Mary, calm down, be a good girl.

> *I must go, I need to be close to him, to think and pray.*
> *I will not pretend everything's all right, you calm down.*

Don't go, Mary. Come back, Mary, Mary ...?

Love is the healer

Blinded, I stumbled to that place of death,
      that rest-in-peace place which holds no rest.
Heart blinded by grief,
eyes blinded by tears.
He had given sight to so many blind in heart and eye
      yet I come here seeking no cure for this blindness.

Deafened, I felt my way to that place of final end,
      that silent place which echoes only fear.
Mind deafened by grief,
ears deafened by the voices of caution.
He opened the ears of so many deaf in mind and ear
      yet I come here seeking no healing for this deafness.

Dumb-founded, I mouthed my holy Sabbath prayers,
      in that un-holiest of places which preys on my grief.
Heart silent for lack of one to love,
voice lost in grief.
He gave voice to the voiceless in heart and life
      yet I come here seeking no words to replace my silence.

Somewhere from within, a scream breaks from my closed throat,
      'They've taken away my Lord!'
I stumble towards the stranger,
gardener in a place stark with barren death,
      'Tell me where they have put him.'

I hear words as mere sound void of meaning, until 'Mary!'
Oh Lord, Oh my God – let me hold you, can it be, is it you, how?

I came for no healing,
I came to dwell and drown in the anguish of my grief,
yet I am healed, my vision is clear,
      my hearing sensitive once more
      and my voice is ready to sing again.

I am healed,
not by time, not by piety, not by ritual,
I am healed by love.
Love beyond death
love beyond time
love beyond all knowing.

Easter prayer

When everything was dark
and it seemed that the sun would never shine again,
your love broke through.

Your love was too strong,
too wide,
too deep
for death to hold.

The sparks cast by your love
dance and spread
and burst forth
with resurrection light.

Gracious God,
we praise you for the light of new life
made possible through Jesus.
We praise you for the light of new life
that shone on the first witnesses of resurrection.
We praise you for the light of new life
that continues to shine in our hearts today.

We pray that the Easter light of life, hope and joy
will live in us each day;
and that we will be bearers of that light
into the lives of others.

                              Amen.

Resurrection appearances

Hearts beating with the rhythm of loss,
    with the anxious, fractured dullness
    of grief, hoping
    against all hope, coping
    with unknowing.

Heads pound with the pain of absence,
    sense and nonsense blend
    in confusion, wondering
    when you will appear again.

Hands form fists of tense anger,
    furious at your coming and
    going, holding on to the ludicrous
    idea of new life.

The rhythm slows and peace
    settles into restless hearts.
The pain points to a loss
    that easy joy would betray.
The tight hands open to reveal
    death's stigma
    dealt a fatal blow.

Wait and see – ascension misgivings

We have watched you,
preaching, reaching, healing,
praying and loving.

You we have seen, taunted,
challenged, threatened
and misunderstood.

We have watched you,
lauded by crowds and anointed
by a woman's love.

You we have seen, betrayed,
battered and condemned
by the power-prompted puppets of law.

We have watched you,
nailed to a cross,
calling Yahweh's absence into presence.

You we have seen, lifted down,
buried in the borrowed tomb,
sealed by rock and guarded.

We have watched you,
risen, with the open-handed reality
of flesh and blood.

You we have seen in the garden,
on the road, by the shore
feeding us with more than food.

We have watched you
ascend, taken into the glory of God,
and we are left empty and abandoned.

What do we watch for now?
'Wait and see' seems an empty sentiment
and patience is a virtue rated by those
who have not known such emptiness.

Pentecost –
making the colours sing

When deep despair casts out all light
and hope is wearing thin;
come, Spirit, dance with gentle grace,
shine through the dullness we embrace
and make the colours sing
and make the colours sing.

When greed dictates that children die
and poverty holds sway;
come, Spirit, burn as living flame,
prompt us to act to end this shame;
cast apathy away
cast apathy away.

When colour, creed, lifestyle or name
cause groundless hate and fear;
come, Spirit, weave a web of peace,
that prejudice and violence cease;
reveal God's purpose here
reveal God's purpose here.

When guilt and fear tear us apart
and faith's a bitter thing;
come, Spirit, dance with gentle grace,
shine through the dullness we embrace
and make God's colours sing
and make God's colours sing.

Tune: Repton
Metre 86886 (& Repeat)

Prayer based on Hebrews 4.14-16

Jesus, Son of God,
our great high priest,
help us pass each test,
each test of faith
each test of endurance
each test of temptation.

Jesus, Son of God,
our great high priest,
help us to approach the throne of grace
boldly
faithfully
expectantly.

Jesus, Son of God,
our great high priest,
help us to hold fast to our confession,
confessing the cross
confessing the resurrection
confessing you as God.

Amen.

Blessings

Gracious God,
as from its source a river finds the sea,
    may we find you, who is both source and destiny.
May we know something of your powerful beauty
    and everything of your intimate love.
May we be the means through which your love
    flows out into the world.
May we know your blessing, now and always.
                                    Amen.

May the voice of the Creator speak to you,
may the healing of the Redeemer release you,
and may the gentle strength of the Sustainer empower you.
                            Amen.

God who is with us each step of the way,
protect those we care for and guide their journeying.
God who is with us at the end of the day,
protect our sleep and grant us good dreams.
God who is with us come what may,
protect our faith and help us to grow.
Father, Son and Holy Spirit,
bless us now and always. Amen.

When I wake and meet the dawn
bless my rising, gracious God.
When I work and when I play
bless my doing, gracious God.
When all is said and all is done
bless my rest, gracious God.

Image acknowledgements

Cover Photo   Pentecost Window at St Paul's Anglican Church, Oswaldtwistle
Permission: Canon Michael Radcliffe. Photo Credit: Sandy Youngson

Frontispiece   Detail from a window at Pluscarden Abbey, Nr Elgin
Permission: Father Camilus. Photo Credit: Sandy Youngson

Chapter 1   Creation Window, Chester Cathedral
Artist: Rosalind Grimshaw. Permission and Photo Credit: Paignton Cowan

Chapter 2   Anniversary Window at Port Gordon Church of Scotland
Permission: Marai Dick – Sessions Clerk. Photo Credit: Sandy Youngson

Chapter 3   Adam and Eve window at Ferryhill Parish Church
Artist: Jennifer-Jane Bayliss, www.jennifer-jane.com
Permission and Photo Credit: Jennifer-Jane and Mike Bayliss

Page 51   Detail from a window at Perth Methodist Church
Permission: Beryl Cowling. Photo Credit: Sandy Youngson

Chapter 4   Detail from a window at Pluscarden Abbey, Nr Elgin
Permission: Father Camilus. Photo Credit: Sandy Youngson

Chapter 5   Detail from a window at St Margaret's, Newlands
Artist, Permission and Photo Credit: John K. Clark, www.glasspainter.com

Chapter 6   Detail from a window at St Petros Kirche, Worms – Herrnshein
Artist, Permission and Photo Credit: John K. Clark, www.glasspainter.com

Chapter 7   HIV Window, at the Medical Library, Royal London Hospital, Whitechapel
Artist: Johannes Schreiter
Permission: Librarian. Photo Credit: Sandy Youngson

Chapter 8   St Gregory window at Pluscarden Abbey, Nr Elgin
Permission: Father Camilus. Photo Credit: Sandy Youngson

Chapter 9   Piper Alpha Memorial Window at Ferryhill Parish Church
Artist: Jennifer-Jane Bayliss, www.jennifer-jane.com
Permission: Jennifer-Jane and Mike Bayliss. Photo Credit: Sandy Youngson

Chapter 10   Detail from the New Testament window at Amberg – Ammersricht
Artist, Permission and Photo Credit: John K. Clark, www.glasspainter.com

Index